More Birds of a Feather Volume Two

NCPA ANTHOLOGY

A collection of fiction and nonfiction animal stories by NCPA authors and poets.

Barbara Barrett, Julie Beyers, Denise Lee Branco, Erin G. Burrell, Scott Charles, Emma Umana Clasberry, Sharon S Darrow, Roberta L. Davis, Kimberly A. Edwards, Elaine Faber, M.L. Hamilton, Bob Irelan, Ronald Javor, Charlene Johnson, Barbara Klide, Elena M. "Ellie" Macaluso, Duncan MacVean D.V.M., Danita Moon, Ellen Osborn, Steve Pastis, Karen A. Phillips, Carolyn Radmanovich, Lisa M. Randolph, Dorothy Rice, Amy Rogers, Cheryl Ann Stapp, Norma Jean Thornton, Judy Vaughan, Christine L. Villa, Gladys Wilburn, & Barbara Young

MORE BIRDS OF A FEATHER: Volume Two

A collection of fiction and nonfiction animal stories by NCPA writers and poets.

Published by
Samati Press
P.O. Box 214673
Sacramento, CA 95821
www.sharonsdarrow.com

This book is independently published by Samati Press in arrangement with individual members of Northern California Publishers & Authors: www.norcalpa.org.

Printed in the United States of America

ISBN: (paperback) 978-1-94-9125-07-8
      (ebook)978-1-949125-08-5

Table of Contents

MARLEY—I'VE GOT TO BE ME..*1*

MY ELK AND PENGUIN STORY..*6*

ANOTHER CHANCE..*11*

RAJU, THE CRYING ELEPHANT..*14*

BRINGING THE CHRISTMAS TREE HOME..*19*

THE ELEPHANT CHAMPION..*25*

THE GREAT ESCAPE..*34*

HAROLD'S SEARCH..*39*

A DIFFERENT KIND OF CHRISTMAS..*50*

CAESAR ON THE THRONE..*62*

ONE MORE STONE..*70*

THE MACABRE MACAQUE..*76*

FRENCHIE – A LOVE STORY..*81*

EACH TIME I DO..*86*

BORN IN A BOAT..*90*

MAXI..*94*

THE SINGING STARS..*100*

LIVE LIKE A KID..*103*

THE ALASKAN ADVENTURE..*106*

ENOUGH OF THE PIG PUNS!..*115*

THE YARD..*118*

THE ETHER SQUIRREL INCIDENT..*123*

INTRODUCTION TO CHICKENESE..*132*

TROPHY SHOT..*139*

ONE GOOD DEED DESERVES ANOTHER..*144*

SENT BY AN ANGEL..*149*

ON THE PORCH WITH MISS LIZZY..*152*

ONE..*158*

HOW TORTOISE FOUND OUT NAMES OF 3 PRINCESSES......................*163*

ALIEN CAT..*172*

ALONG CAME RYAN...THE LITTLE GOSLING KING..............................*176*

MARLEY—I'VE GOT TO BE ME

AS TOLD TO BOB IRELAN

Hi, Marley here.

No, not the protagonist in the book, *Marley and Me*, or the star in the movie of the same name. I have my own identity and I am special in my own way. Or at least that's what my "people parents" and other humans who know me say.

I'm not quite as handsome as that other Marley. I grayed around my snout when I was just a couple of years old and my coat has always been a bit coarse and gnarly. But whatever I lack in looks, I make up for in personality. And, darn it, I'm still a purebred Golden Retriever and I'm named after Bob Marley, the legendary King of Reggae.

I was adopted when I was a couple of months old. I remember it well. I was in one of those kiddie pools with my canine brothers and sisters when a woman (my future human mom, Melissa) and a pre-teenager (my future human brother, Jonathan) appeared. Jonathan picked me up and, after I wouldn't stop wiggling and kissing him, said, "I want this one."

What I didn't know until they took me home was that there was another dog who looked a lot like me. He was (still is) named Jagger – after the Rocker Mick Jagger. So, we became "brothers" and best pals. Jagger is a few months older than I am and, it pains me to admit, he, too, is better looking. In fact, everything that's handsome about Goldens, he's got.

I learned we were successors to two previous Goldens: Dylan (for Bob Dylan) and Santana (for Carlos Santana). I guess we come in pairs. What's all this about musicians and dogs?

Jagger and I are both 12 now (I think that works out to somewhere in the 80's in human years) but Jon (my human dad), Melissa and Jonathan contend I still act like a puppy. They cite things like my going outside for a couple of minutes and then bounding back in, jumping around, and greeting them or anyone else as if I haven't seen them in years. Or trying to climb up in Grandpa Bob's lap when he's trying to watch a football game. Or, best of all, using my snout to suddenly and forcefully jar loose someone's grip on an hors d'oeuvre, chip, or any other tasty morsel. Sure, I might get scolded, but most of the time the reward outweighs the risk.

Sadly, Jagger is showing his age. He doesn't want to wrestle anymore. We used to really get into it. He was bigger and stronger and loved to pin me down. I miss that. I also miss him tugging at the neckerchief I often wore after a bath. He'd grab hold of it and yank me all around the living room.

Jon and Melissa were worried awhile back that Jagger might be on his last legs. He'd lost a lot of weight and become lethargic. But after they quit giving him the medicine he hated, he bounced back. He's not his old self; I doubt he ever will be. But he's put on some pounds, is more energetic, and is doing okay. I surely like having him around.

A role reversal has taken place with Jagger and me. Whereas I used to follow his lead, especially when we were in an unfamiliar setting, he now follows mine; it makes me feel good that he trusts me. Lately, on a few occasions, I have run upstairs in the middle of the night to awaken Jon and Melissa and tell them Jagger needs to go out. We're good dogs and know where to take care of our business.

We have a beautiful yard with a pool and spa. Summers are hot in Sacramento, and I love taking a dip whenever the mood strikes. My favorite is getting in the spa and resting my chin on the tile edge. Sometimes Jon hollers at me. I guess it's because he's just swept the pool and, truth be told, I do shed more than a little bit. Or maybe it's because he and Melissa are a bit touchy about my wanting to charge into the house right after jumping out of the spa, trailing puddles of water in my wake.

Our neighbors have dogs. We bark at each other through nearly solid fences where the vertical boards allow only narrow views. Some people believe our yapping constitutes territorial warnings. It's not that. It's just our way of communicating – one canine neighbor to another. People tend to overanalyze things.

I'm told I crave attention. I can sit up, balanced on my back legs for long periods so long as my chest is rubbed. And don't sit down unless you want me to join you. Melissa says I'm needy, but isn't that what makes dogs like me so special? Who wants an aloof, independent dog? If you want those qualities, maybe you ought to consider getting a cat.

What I like best is going to the family cabin in the Sierra. I love the walks with Jon, Melissa, and Jagger, where I sniff and mark every tree until I no longer can. And the winters there…they are the greatest. Sometimes the snow is deeper than I am tall, so I have to hold my head up and hop rather than try to run. Fetching snowballs is challenging because they either disappear deep into the snow or disintegrate as soon as I grab hold of them.

Oh, I almost forgot. I'm not a picky eater. In fact, I can't think of anything I won't try. A lot of what I eat tastes the same because, while Jagger chews and swallows, I wolf down so fast the taste buds don't have time to activate. The exception is carrots, the baby ones, not the long, curvy ones with a clump of green on the top. They require some chewing. I love their taste, and Melissa keeps my very own supply in a jar in the fridge. All she has to ask is, "Marley, you want some carrots?" and I know to run straight for the kitchen. The same goes for ice cubes; I love to crunch them.

One more thing. Melissa planted a garden again this year. I don't bother the veggies, though I'm sure they're very good. But I surreptitiously help pick the strawberries, often before they are ripe. They are delicious.

Bottom line, life is good – with one exception: fireworks. I know it's silly and I know they're pretty much confined to Independence Day and New Year's Eve, but the blasts and high-pitched whistles scare the bejeebers out of me. Despite my breeding, I clearly wasn't cut out for hunting and loud noises. Jon and Melissa have tried everything to comfort me. Tranquilizers, confinement to a room with blinds drawn, loud music to drown out the offending sound. None of it works. I can still hear the noise and I hate it. We dogs prefer to make our own noise. It's called barking.

I know I'm lucky. I could be one of those dogs you see in the Humane Society commercials on TV. I can't stand to watch them. They are either deserted, or chained outside in the cold, or physically injured. Instead, I'm blessed to have the companionship of Jagger and the love of Jon, Melissa, Jonathan and Grandpa.

Yep, I appreciate all that is given to me so generously. In return, I try to show my gratitude by spreading happiness and unconditional love every waking hour. Based on the feedback I get, I give myself an "A."

Bob Irelan's commitment to writing began in earnest when he majored in journalism at the University of Maryland, and grew steadily from there.

Following 10 years of newspaper and magazine reporting and editing, including stints at The Wall Street Journal and Nation's Business magazine in Washington, DC, he spent 32 years in public relations for a Fortune 500 family of companies. As a corporate officer, he directed the companies' internal and external communications for the last 12 of those years.

In retirement, Bob taught public relations courses for two years at University of the Pacific and five years at University of California, Davis, Extension.

Irelan authored the novel, *Angel's Truth – One teenager's quest for justice*, which took second place in Fiction at NCPA's 25th Book Awards in 2019.

Bob lives in Rancho Murieta, California, with his cat, Jocko, who he wrote about in NCPA's *Birds of a Feather* Anthology.

MY ELK AND PENGUIN STORY

STEVE PASTIS

So I'm driving to Idaho with an elk I just met. He's not saying much and I'm starting to feel a little uneasy. I met him at a mini-mart down in a town in northeastern Nevada. He was standing in front of me in line, going on and on about the new Mars bar that he was buying and it sounded like it was worth a try. He saved my place in line so I could go to the candy aisle and get one.

Seems he was trying to get back to Idaho. That's where his parents live and where the elk he was supposed to marry was when he left three years ago to try his luck in Hollywood.

Everybody is looking for something in life, at least that's been my observation. I developed a special respect for those who actually reach for what they want, even if they find themselves going back home with their tail between their legs.

Me, I was on the road just hoping to see life more clearly. I wanted to get a better idea what it was that I should be looking for. This elk was a few steps ahead of me in his quest so I offered him a ride. I figured maybe I could learn something from him.

Anyway, we left the mini-mart and headed north. Like I said, he wasn't talking much. We ate our Mars bars and listened to some Dylan.

We were each tangled up in our own thoughts when we passed three penguins on the side of the road. The elk and I looked at each other and I think it was the elk that first theorized that the penguins were hitchhiking. It should have been obvious, I suppose, but you get conditioned to expect hitchhikers to have a thumb up when you pass. You forget that those without thumbs sometimes need rides too.

We turned back and soon I was driving north with an elk in the front passenger seat and three penguins in the back seat. I was glad the car was rented.

So I am thinking about everything I know about elks because it occurs to me that this elk may be naming our three new South Pole pals breakfast, lunch, and dinner. I don't think this is likely, but I figure this may be a good time to bring out the box of Triscuits I had hidden under the seat.

So he's munching on a Triscuit, and the Dylan CD has played through. I figure it's a good time for everyone to introduce themselves. We all seem to have a handle on each other's species, but other than the three penguins, nobody knows anybody else's name.

The elk introduces himself as Clark, and the three penguins are Maureen, Sunray, and Ethel. The elk's eyes lit up when he realized we were traveling with three females. He started flirting and incorporated all of his elk charms into his effort.

The three penguins didn't say much but they giggled a lot. Just then, my cell phone rang. Nobody else was on the highway, so I figured I could answer it without risking getting a ticket.

It was my wife. She wanted to know how my journey of self-discovery was going. Before I could answer, she heard female giggling and became rather concerned.

"No need to fear, my dear wife," I said. "Clark the elk and I are driving three penguins to Idaho."

There was a long pause. It occurred to me that she might not believe me. I may have used an elk and penguin story before.

"I don't believe you," she said rather sternly. "You've used an elk and penguin story before."

Clark seemed to understand my problem. He grabbed my phone and gave out a loud elk mating call. My wife was stunned. The three penguins were suddenly intrigued. There was a loud thud on the roof and we passed the Idaho border.

It was a rather eventful moment.

Clark used my cell phone to take and send a photo of the penguins to my wife. She told me to call her when I got to a hotel room, and said goodbye.

I was curious about the thud on the roof, but once again I was happy that I was driving a rented car.

I pulled off at the next exit. There was a market there and the penguins wanted to stop for the new Mars bar that they had heard good things about. I studied the large indent in the roof of the car.

When we got out of the car, we couldn't help noticing an elk was stretched out on the roof of the car. Clark recognized her immediately. It was Delia, his fiancée. She hopped off the roof of the car and the two of them pranced out into the woods. I knew I wouldn't see Clark again.

The three penguins each grabbed a new Mars bar and walked over to get cold drinks. One of them, I think it was Sunray, decided on a Sierra Mist. She opened the cooler door and they all quickly realized that they had found something truly special – not the drink, the cooler.

The boxes of cans and bottles were in disarray in the cooler, but the penguins didn't seem to care. They were happy to find a cool place to stay for a few moments. Actually, they really didn't want to come out.

Sanjib, the market manager, walked from behind the front counter to tell us to leave. I was ready to leave, but Maureen, Sunray, and Ethel didn't want to go. They were where they wanted to be.

Sanjib said he had to go back to the front counter because it was too cold for him to stand by the cooler. He repeated that we should leave.

I followed him to the front counter and offered him a proposition. If the penguins could stay where they were, they could keep the cooler tidy and all the shelves stocked, and he could pay them with cans of tuna fish and Mars candy bars.

Sanjib liked the idea and thanked me by giving me a few of the new Mars bars.

I explained things to the penguins. They were happy

with the new arrangement and I was soon back on the road.

As I traveled through Idaho and then back through Utah and Nevada again on my way home, I would make other stops and have other adventures, but the way I negotiated a deal between Sanjib and the penguins would be the most important part of my journey. I discovered a talent that I didn't know I had.

So, even though there is nothing on my resume that shows any experience for the position, this is why I really believe I could do a great job handling your company's labor relations.

Steve Pastis has written for the *Valley Voice*, *The Good Life*, *Greek Accent*, *Farm News*, *Custom Boat & Engine*, *Baseball Cards*, *Circus*, *Rock Fever*, *Occidental Magazine*, *Destination Visalia*, *South Valley Networking*, *Hellenic Calendar*, and *Cool and Strange Music*.

His stories have been published in *The Journal of Experimental Fiction*, *Signs of Life*, and *Gargoyle*. Three of his short story collections, *Fables for the Clarinet*, *Ten Good Reasons to Fix that Airplane*, and *Elk and Penguin Stories*, are available on Amazon.

ANOTHER CHANCE

CHERYL ANNE STAPP

He was just a little dog, with a Pomeranian's upright, tufted ears and a dachshund's short-legged body; aging and thin and always hungry, reduced to sniffing out discarded food wrappers behind fast food joints.

Once upon a time, he couldn't remember exactly when, he had been fed and stroked by human hands until—perhaps—he ventured outside too far one day and got lost, or was turned out to fend for himself when his human family couldn't keep him anymore. He didn't waste too much time trying to puzzle out why he was on his own now: the bigger issue was simply survival from one day to the next, grasping each opportunity that appeared. He remembered those happy times, though, and knew those alpha-beings who stood on two legs were a source of food, so he always offered friendly, hopeful greetings whenever he saw one.

Maybe he was a bit *too* friendly, hanging about a backyard where he wasn't wanted. Or maybe he was perceived as too dangerous when he warned pets and other street dogs away from morsels of food with a deep-throated, bared-teeth snarl.

Probably, it was those very teeth that frightened cautious homeowners. His front teeth were so crowded and crooked that he couldn't properly close his lips over them, saddling him with the sneer of an aggressor even as his wagging tail signaled benign intentions. Someone, fearing an attack on their ankles or just tired of shooing off a little beggar, alerted the dreaded dog catcher.

Animal Control came and scooped him up from Sacramento's streets, and thrust him into a cage in a big building with hundreds of other frightened animals. He had no collar, no imbedded chip, and no one who came to claim him.

The humans who poked at him, who forced his jaws open to inspect those fearsome teeth, concluded that he was likely twelve—an old dog, with possibly only four more years to live. In the pet adoption sweepstakes, the little guy's age was a distinct disadvantage, coupled with certain negative traits attributed to his breed mix: not good with children; thought to be stubborn; barks too much.

On the positive side, the characteristics of both breeds also meant he was clever, playful, sociable, and loyal. Best of all, except for his dental issues and a minor eye infection, he was alert, healthy and sweet-tempered...so he was given another chance.

The Sacramento shelter contacted Muttville, a non-profit organization that rescues and finds homes for senior dogs.

The staff at Muttville accepted him into their cage-free facility in San Francisco, where they gave him a thorough evaluation, a case number, and a temporary name. He quickly made new friends with thirty or so other rescued senior canines, and his quirky charm captured the hearts of dozens of volunteers who took him on daily walks along city sidewalks. He was warm and safe, fed and petted and praised at Muttville (really, he told himself, he had won a starring role) yet somehow, he knew the place wasn't permanent, that an even better life was still out there somewhere.

That better life, his best life, began when he was adopted by a couple who were classified as senior citizens like himself; vigorous and caring folks he loved from the first day. Who had he loved before? In dreams, he saw shadowy faces from the past. But that was then...in his long-ago life. The new ones were his people now—his future—and age was just a number because it was never too late to make a new beginning.

Cheryl Anne Stapp writes nonfiction California history. A native Sacramentan, she graduated from California State University, Northridge, while working in the entertainment industry. During her last five years in Los Angeles, she was a contributing editor to *Working World*, a regional magazine—then returned home in 2000 to marry a great guy she had known since high school. Cheryl lives in Sacramento with her husband and their beloved pets, facilitates a monthly breakfast meeting for writers, and volunteers as a docent at Sutter's Fort State Historic Park. Website https://cherylannestapp.com

She is the author of: *Rise, Ruin & Restoration – A History of Sutter's Fort* ; *Before The Gold Rush - The Sinclairs of Rancho del Paso 1840-1849* ; *Disaster & Triumph: Sacramento Women, Gold Rush Through the Civil War*; *Sacramento Chronicles - A Golden Past*, and *The Stagecoach in Northern California: Rough Rides, Gold Camps, and Daring Drivers*.

RAJU, THE CRYING ELEPHANT

L.M. RANDOLPH

Why would an elephant cry, you ask? Like we humans, does he cry for joy or pain? For love or heartache? That is a question indeed. If you would genuinely like to know, sit, allow me to tell you the story of Raju, the crying elephant.

*   *   *

They tricked him. Lured away with sweet mangos, the little elephant followed the Mahout. At first, it was a delightful treat. Such attention he was given as they used a boar-bristled hairbrush to stroke his body. He trumpeted happily as they scratched behind his large ears. He did not notice the man as he shackled Raju's feet with chains. Did not notice the other men as they led his mother away. He was dazed with happiness as he took yet another mango in his trunk, put it in his mouth and chewed, delicious mango juices dripping down his chin. This was wonderful, but now he wanted the comfort of his mother. As he attempted to walk away, something bit painfully, metal spikes chewed into the tender skin of his ankles. Raju panicked. Trumpeting loudly, scared and confused, he tried again and again to free himself. It was too late; there was nothing she could do to save him. His loving mother whisked away, never to be seen again. And so, began the life of Raju, the crying elephant.

*   *   *

Raju ambled slowly along the busy streets of the Indian

village, begging for food, and money, as his new mahout, number twenty and seven, sat upon his mighty shoulders. He longed for the days when sweet fruits filled his belly. Now his days were filled with bitterness, and intolerable cruelty.

As if the man read his thoughts, he struck Raju behind the ears; a long hard stick with a metal hook dug into his flesh. After so many years, he no longer cried out, nearly immune to its discomfort. It was part of his performance. The hook pierced his skin no less than one hundred times per day, leaving him raw and bloody. This was his cue to shake his head back and forth, entertaining the crowds of people watching. Several hard kicks to the back of his head, and up he went on two legs, begging. The people cheered and threw rupees.

Days grew into nights, nights into days. For Raju, they were never-ending, as were the terrible conditions under which he lived. Cruelty was visited upon him every moment of his life since that fateful day he was stolen away from his mother. The heavy chains rattled with every step. After fifty years, he barely noticed the painful swelling, hardly noticed the trickling of blood down his legs. He was given food of little nutritional value, to fill the emptiness of his stomach. He picked strings of hay out of the mud that was his bed. Hunger a constant companion; some days he ate nothing at all. A bull elephant of his size should weigh five-thousand kilograms, Raju was a grossly underweight two-thousand kilograms.

This night, he lay down, for what was possibly the last time. He was bone-tired, weary beyond words, his desire to live lost. The mahout beat Raju unmercifully to keep him obedient, a broken spirit. Too weak to fight back, accepting blow after blow to his body, Raju let out a low elephant rumble, this night's beating finally finished. With a deep sigh, he closed his eyes and fell into a deep, dreamless sleep.

*   *   *

His slumber disturbed; Raju reluctantly opened his eyes among a mass of confusion. He wanted silence, wanted to be left alone, wanted to die, peacefully.

Angry voices. People were shouting. Some carried torches, the firelight reflected in his weary brown eyes. Nothing frightened him anymore. Dozens of people surrounded him, the voice of his owner, the loudest and angriest of them all. He had no idea why so many were there. It was dark time; his torture usually began at first light.

It was a daring and dangerous rescue attempt. Unbeknownst to Raju or his owner, they were being followed. For months, each instance of abuse was documented by a team of officials, the facts presented in a court of law. The judge issued the court order post-haste for Raju's removal, such was the level of brutality. Six police officers, twenty members from the Department of Forestry, four veterinarians and wildlife experts from the British based Wildlife SOS, held back the angry mahout.

Their anger matched his. "You, sir, are under arrest for the torture and cruelty of this animal. You have the right to remain silent…" the police officer stated, while the other handcuffed the belligerently outraged mahout.

It was he who was now in chains.

They worked furiously to free the elephant of his manacles. The barbaric devices of torture fell away one by one. For the first time since a baby elephant, Raju was free of shackles. Fifty years. Fifty years it had taken. His trunk reached for his mangled ankles, to find nothing there.

The veterinarians tended the bloodied wounds, administering antibiotics to prevent further infection of Raju's many gory gashes. He sat up; just sat there for several minutes, then a deep resonating rumble came from his chest. Everyone froze, afraid of what he might do next. After so many years of abuse and torture, who knew what he was capable of? Who could blame him for being a savage beast? The wildlife experts were ready with a sedative to calm him. They waited in anticipation. Raju began to move again, to his knees first, then standing on all four feet. And then, the most miraculous thing happened.

Tear drops rolled down the face of the majestic pachyderm. Raju the elephant was crying, to the amazement of all who witnessed the event. Tears of freedom, freedom from bondage, a life of torture that he would never suffer again. They too cried along with this massive beast of burden. So again, you ask, why would an elephant cry? Is it from joy or pain, love or heartache? I believe it can be from all these things.

* * *

At approximately one-minute past midnight on the fourth of July, two-thousand fifteen, Raju the crying elephant, was rescued and delivered to the Elephant Conservation and Care Center, a sanctuary for abused elephants, located in the city of Mathura in northern India. Five-hundred kilometers now separate Raju from the horrific life he once knew.

Upon arrival, Raju was greeted by the "Herd of Hope" consisting of several female elephants rescued under similar circumstances. Laxmi, Chanchal and Sai Geeta flapped their ears—an expression of joy, and touched him with their trunks, in welcome.

With love and patience, he has learned to trust humans. Proper medical care and a diet rich in nutrition, including the delicious delights of sugar cane, apples and yes, an endless supply of mangos, Raju is today at a healthy robust weight.

Celebrating his fourth year of liberty with his new elephant family, Raju has adjusted well to a life of freedom, spending most of his time in a pool of water where he sometimes falls asleep for hours on end, finally at peace.

Lisa M. Randolph, an aspiring children's book writer, goes by the pen name L.M. Randolph. Her first action-adventure series *The Wildlife Divas Adventure Team* and short story *Raju the Crying Elephant*, tackles the subject of Wildlife Conservation and Endangered Species. Her real-life adventures have taken her to four of seven continents of the world. Her fascinating hobby of 'Rock Hunting' for semi-precious stones has sent her exploring mountains reaching heights up to 8000 feet, to valley floors of ancient seabed's hunting for trilobite fossils. Don't be surprised when meeting her to find her pockets filled with an interesting array of rocks, crystals and gemstones.

Lisa resides in Elk Grove, California with two small rescue dogs, Rose (a terrier-mix) and Petal (a teacup chihuahua) and admits to being their emotional support human. They've inspired her upcoming children's book series, *The Adventures of an Ugly Dog in a Tutu*.

BRINGING THE CHRISTMAS TREE HOME

JUDITH VAUGHAN

December, 1955

No other third grader was having lunch with her Daddy. I hated pinto beans. So, when they appeared on the school lunch menu, I'd ask Daddy to take me to lunch. That December day, he picked me up from Gallinas Street School. After a short drive up Grand Avenue, we settled into a cozy booth at the Home Café in Las Vegas, New Mexico.

The waitress wore a hairnet. "Judy, what'll it be? I know you don't need a menu."

Daddy said. "How about pinto beans?"

"Hah," I said, snorting like a horse. "I'll take the hot beef sandwich, on white bread, laid out open face on the plate, easy on the gravy."

The waitress laughed. "No child's plate?" She and Daddy were grinning at my expense.

"Don't forget the knife and fork," I said.

The hot beef cost sixty-five cents. Daddy picked the hamburger and fries for fifty-five cents. Our drinks, a Coke for me and coffee for him were each a nickel.

As we waited for our meals, the wall calendar over the counter caught my eye. In the picture for December, a cowboy on horseback was dragging an evergreen tree through a snowy landscape. He had emerged from the forest on the left side of the picture and was about to ride through a field. His Collie dog trotted beside the horse, and in the distance, smoke wreathed the chimney of a log house. I got up and walked to the counter to read the caption: *Bringing the*

Christmas Tree Home.

"Let's get our Christmas tree this weekend," I said as I slipped back into the booth. "We can ride to Water Canyon."

As we ate our sandwiches, we planned the outing. I would be like that picture tomorrow, dragging the Christmas tree behind my horse, Babe, our dog Cindy trotting beside us.

On Saturday, the ground was still frosty when Daddy and I saddled up. Babe and I cantered past the old Victorian hotel at Montezuma, where we lived, five miles from Las Vegas. Daddy's horse, Lady, was a walking horse – she could walk as fast as Babe cantered. The bucksaw clattered against Daddy's saddle. I carried an old lariat, soft from age, coiled and tied to the horn of the child-sized western saddle. We made good time as we entered Water Canyon.

"What a joke," I said. "It has no water at all."

"It's the dry season. See how steep the banks are? It floods every spring and washes out the road," Daddy said.

Cindy, an overweight Labrador Retriever, lagged behind. We waited for her to catch up and walked the horses slowly. The land rose and the canyon narrowed, surrounded by forest.

"That's a nice tree," I said. I swung off Babe and inspected it, fingering its narrow needles and inhaling its holiday fragrance

"It's an Engelman Spruce," said Daddy. "Look at the color. It's often confused with its cousin, the Colorado Blue Spruce."

It was not as full as the calendar tree, but no matter. Trees were leaner in dry New Mexico. We tied the horses to stout pines, and Daddy sawed the spruce down with the bucksaw. He looped the end of the old lariat around its slim trunk and tied a knot above a lower branch.

"A soft rope allows a tight knot. We don't want it slipping off the trunk," Daddy said.

I was ready to jump up on Babe and dally the rope around the saddle horn. I'd take the tree home just like the calendar cowboy on the wall of the Home Cafe.

But Cindy began whining and lay down at my feet. I petted her. "Cindy, get up. What's the matter?" She groaned and flopped over on her side. I pulled at Daddy's sleeve. "There's something wrong with Cindy,"

He looked down at the dog. A doctor first, a human doctor second, and an eye specialist third, he dropped to his hands and knees, put his ear on her chest, and listened to the fat dog's heart.

He stood up. Bit his lip. Looked at me.

"Stay here with Cindy. She's had a heart attack." He put his denim jacket over her. "I'll ride to the stable and drive the pick-up back up the road to get her and you."

My face must have given me away. "Don't be scared," he said, "but be patient. I have to ride all the way to the stable, and it will be a slow drive back in the truck." He sighed and looked down the road. "Somehow I have to let Mother know what's happened."

I sat on the ground and comforted Cindy. She stopped moaning and licked my hand. I thought of Daddy galloping back to the stable. Lady would be nervous without Babe. Water Canyon was no joke now. The two ruts of the road where I waited mocked the canyon's wide dry mouth back in Montezuma. Wet spots left over from the summer thunderstorms had added to the runoff water. Would Daddy and our Chevy make it back or slip off the road into the muddy drainage?

Babe stomped and whinnied when Daddy rode off. I had two animals to take care of. Cindy fell asleep. I picked some dry grass to calm Babe who desperately wanted to leave with Lady. I thought about wolves and decided New Mexico didn't have any. I shivered as the trees and the mountains shaded me and my pets. My teacher had talked about the short days of December; how Christmas and Hanukkah were festivals of light to lift people's spirits during the season when nights were longer than days. Would Daddy be back before dark?

Finally, I heard the gears of the Chevy grind up the last

grade. Daddy made it. He gave me a hug. "How's Cindy?" He offered our dog a pan of water. She lapped a swallow then looked at him. Where were the bright eyes I was used to? She yelped a single cry as he set her on the bench seat in the cab of the pickup. When Daddy moved the water next to her, she raised her head and drank a little more. She groaned and seemed to fall asleep. He put his hand on her still body and turned to me.

"Judy, Cindy might not make it. She's an old dog. Let's get the tree loaded and take our dog home."

I fought tears. Cindy? Old? I couldn't remember a time without her.

He hugged me and confessed he had worried about me, too. I didn't feel so much like a sissy. Then I hopped into the truck bed and steadied the tree trunk as Daddy lifted the Christmas tree. He pushed it all the way into the pick-up and tied it down with the lariat. The calendar picture wasn't going to happen.

"I'll go in second gear," he said. "It'll seem fast, but I can't let the truck get stuck."

He gave me a boost onto my horse's back. "Babe's hungry, don't let her go too fast. You know how she loves to run home."

Racing down the canyon, I saw a shadow beside me. It started from Babe's feet and soon made a cloud-like silhouette of truck, horse, and rider as it rose from the road and clung loping to the hill.

I felt Babe check her footing as she picked the best way out of the darkening canyon. Every few seconds, my gaze found the shape again. It blurred and faded in the setting sun. If I could trace the dancing shadow and fill in the muted colors – the blue pickup bouncing down a muddy road with a Christmas tree in the back and a girl following on her strawberry roan cow pony – I would have a picture. As the shadow disappeared, the image grew inside me. An inner voice added its comment. "That calendar cowboy has nothing to do with you. Your canyon, Daddy, Babe, and a fat old dog are truer and more beautiful than the calendar picture you envied."

Cindy poked her head out the window of the real truck. She barked as we passed a house near our barn. She was feeling better.

A few days later, resplendent in colored lights and glass balls, the tree spread its limbs over the Christmas gift for me, a little pressed-tin western town with molded rubber cowboys and horses in natural poses. I recognized the set from the Montgomery Ward catalog I had perused since Thanksgiving, the pages showing toys dogeared with my wishes. The Western Town Set cost $5.95. It must have been ordered weeks ago. A string tag attached to a bow-legged rubber cowboy read, "To Judy, from Mother and Daddy." Someone had added to the bottom, "And for bravery, from Cindy."

The Labrador lived another three years, but she never went with us on another trail ride, even to pick out a Christmas tree.

Judy Vaughan grew up in Northern New Mexico, engrossed in her father's horse breeding hobby. She left the family ranch for boarding school in Colorado and then attended Carleton College and the University of New Mexico School of Medicine. Judy has composed stories, mostly on horseback, since childhood, and began to hone the craft of writing ten years ago after forty years practicing medicine. She lives in Elk Grove, California, and writes with Elk Grove Writers and Artists.

Works in progress include her New Mexico memoir, *Strawberry Roan*. Her stories have placed in the last two short story contests of the Sacramento Branch of the California Writers Club.

Contact her at jfbvaughan@comcast.net.

THE ELEPHANT CHAMPION

GLADYS UNIMUKE WILBURN

I loved sharing early mornings with my grandmother. I would watch as she shuffled into the kitchen, always wearing her worn-out house slippers and her Pepto Bismol colored chenille bathrobe.

Standing in front of our old-fashioned cooking stove, Grandmother would begin to cook my favorite breakfast: oatmeal. As a special treat, she'd add a large slice of sweet yellow butter and a big clump of brown sugar to the pot of creamy delight. I focused on every movement she made. She stood, with her large wooden spoon in hand, stirring the mixture.

With a smile on my face, I half giggled and asked, "Grandma, do you love me?" I knew the answer to the question, but I just loved hearing her say the words.

"Why are you asking questions like that so early this morning?"

"No reason," I answered.

"Yes, Gladys Jean, I LOVE YOU," she replied. "Now, time is passing. Hurry up and finish your oatmeal. You are going to be late for class."

I slid from the plastic-covered chair that was stationed beneath the kitchen table and made my way to the living room. Grandmother had placed my Red-faced Indian tablet, yellow No.2 pencil, and my green car coat on top of the coffee table. I put them in my book bag and made my way out the door for school.

*   *   *

Ms. Robb, my third-grade teacher was very controlling and strict. She would march up and down the aisles of the classroom with a large red paddle, swaddled in the corner of her folded arms. "I run a tight ship," she would express in a loud voice.

Standing in front of us, she began pounding on the top of an empty desk. "Attention, attention class. Our dear principal, Mr. Woodard, has generously added the third-grade classes to this year's art festival. Our class will enter a mural. The theme for this year's project will be My Favorite Animal."

The announcement seemed to be a direct gift from heaven to me because I loved to draw. Most of all, I loved drawing elephants. In that second, I knew what I would be entering in the project.

The huge, fat bodies of elephants remind me of big, bouncy balloons that sail along as the air catches and moves them through the sky. Bumpety, Bump, Bump, Bump.

Their magnificent, round wrinkled legs remind me of small African drums. First leg down, beat number one. Second leg down, beat two. Beat, beat, beat as they stride majestically along the Earth.

I love to watch a mother elephant caring for her little offspring. On sudden impulse, she moves to connect, head-to–head, with her little one. Making high pitched groans and squeaks, she assures her baby that he is safe.

 I began dreaming of riding an elephant. My small hands would hold on tightly to a particular fold in his neck. Up and down I would move as the hairy patches of his skin rubbed against my thighs. For now, though, I have to settle for my elephant hat and purse.

A loud thundering voice interrupted my reverie. "Stop your daydreaming, Gladys Jean," Ms. Robb ordered. "Are you here with us?" she questioned.

"Who would like to help pass out the art supplies?" I was not Ms. Robbs' favorite student. I was always "too" – too talkative, too jumpy, too, too, too! I tried to stay away from any outrageous actions. I never wanted to draw any attention to myself. I would not be raising my hand.

MiJean Smith was selected to help pass out the art supplies and papers. Our teacher took the left side of the classroom and MiJean supplied the right.

Ms. Robb was formidable, carrying her red paddle along with boxes of assorted color crayons and the stiff packs of school art paper, in her arms.

My desk was located in the last row on the left side of the classroom. Eagerly, I awaited Ms. Robb's arrival. "Here you go," she said, as she laid a complete set of art supplies on my desk.

I ran my small, short fingers over the cheap, textured craft paper. This pleasant feeling helped to prepare my fingers for drawing. First, I drew a large circle. One large body appeared on the paper. Yes, perfect, I thought. Next, I artfully drew a medium-sized circle and attached it to the body.

One section of my drawing seemed to be out of sync, so I reached over to retrieve my gum eraser and began to remove the mistake. There suddenly appeared a small collection of eraser scraps and I lightly swept the pieces away. The middle-sized circle, once completed and corrected, became the head. Looks great, I thought.

I added large legs and a tiny little tail. Several swift moves, and I was finished. It only took a few seconds to complete the project. After I made the final details to the picture, a fullness and sense of achievement settled inside my chest. I should win the prize, I thought. And when I win the prize, Ms. Robb will have to like me

"Oh, Ms. Robb, Ms. Robb!" I began waving my hands in the air, in an attempt to get her attention.

"What is it?" she replied in a rude voice, from across the room.

"I'm finished," I joyfully replied.

Never turning to face me, she answered, "I will be there in a few seconds."

After a long wait, Ms. Robb made her way towards my desk. Making an effort to review my work, she moved close to me. Her large red paddle was still in her folded arms.

"Well…," she said slowly. "This looks okay, but there needs to be a few little changes to make your elephant good enough to put in the festival." This news made my heart overjoyed.

"You know, Gladys," she started, "Elephants are a mighty breed. I am sure you would want to show him in his best light. So, I think it's a good idea to make a few changes to your work."

Changes? What changes could she be speaking of? What elephant was she talking about? My elephant was perfect.

I kept quiet.

She moved her body closer to my little desk. "Well," she began again. "The tail is too short. There are other problems as well, but let's just correct the tail problem first, then we will go from there."

In that moment, I felt all the air leave my lungs. I took a deep breath, then began to make *her* changes to my beautiful elephant. My gum eraser helped remove any traces of the tail that displeased Ms. Robb.

"Ms. Robb, Ms. Robb," I pestered her peace again.

"What is it now?" she replied from another student's desk.

"I finished the tail," I said in a low tone.

"I will be there in a few seconds," she said in a firm voice. Her tone made me feel dejected. Patiently awaiting her return, I sat, hoping to receive her approval of the changes I made. She seemed to be in no hurry though. In her own time, she returned to my desk.

"The tail is okay now, but there are other changes you need to make. The legs are too small, the ears aren't large enough. Have you ever seen an elephant before?" she questioned. I did not answer. How could she even ask me that question?

"Are you retarded?" she screamed loud enough to draw

the attraction of the class. "Has that big, fat braid you wear on top of your head every day made you brain deficient?" she added. I remained quiet. Hearing her harsh words made me even more determined to create the elephant she visualized.

Ms. Robb dictated fourteen suggestions and I made fourteen changes. I drew and erased so many times that several large holes appeared in the thin art paper. The elephant had taken on the shape of something crude and ugly. My beautiful animal had all but disappeared. He was no longer a stately picture of a superior being. His portrait was now a sickly, lumpy mess of unrelated lines and circles.

"Ms. Robb," I called out for the last time. "I think I am finished." She made her final march to my desk, for her last inspection.

"WHAT IS THIS? Look at all those holes. I can't use this mess. Ball it up and throw it in the trash. Throw that mess away!" she demanded.

The school bell rang and the other students jumped up from their seats. Everyone made their way towards the classroom door, except me. Ms. Robb was just as eager to exit the room; gathering her belongings, she swiftly left the building without saying goodbye.

Sitting alone and feeling completely dejected, I opened my book bag and placed the torn, holey, elephant picture inside.

I needed to get home.

I needed Grandma.

Confused, ashamed, and disappointed, I struggled to walk home. Each step brought moments of deep breathing, nose snuffling, and large crocodile tears. It was truly a relief to finally arrive home to safety. I went directly to my room and threw myself on the bed, giving myself permission to release an ocean of tears. I was so deeply involved in my sadness that I never heard my grandmother enter the bedroom.

She positioned herself near the foot of my bed. "Are you crying?" she asked in a soft voice.

"Yes," I answered, still sobbing.

"What's wrong?"

I gulped and stammered, "Nuh-nuh-nothing."

Placing her hip on the side of my bed and, leaning forward, she gingerly placed her hands-on top of my foot, and started to move her hands back and forth across the top of my toes. That always made me feel safe and loved.

"Well, there must be something wrong. Whatever the problem is, it seems to have made you upset enough to cry," she said in her kind voice.

There were a few seconds of silence. "Ms. Robb was mean to me," I answered in a matter-of-fact attitude.

Correcting her posture, Grandmother stood up and folded her arms across her chest. "How was she mean?"

I began relating all the details of the incident involving my picture. After patiently listening to my story, Grandmother asked, "Did you throw your picture away?"

I took a deep breath, and in a whiney voice I answered, "Nooo." I got up and made my way to the table near the bed. My book bag containing the crumpled Elephant drawing was on top of the table. Slowly, I unfolded the picture and gave it to Grandmother. Her expert gaze scanned each part of the lumpy, ragged paper. She made a low "Hmmm" sound.

She finished reviewing my sad rendition of the elephant. "Boy, you really made some big holes." She placed the brown mess into my hands. "Put it back in your bag," she directed.

"Baby," she began, speaking in a low, slow, comforting voice, which reached my aching heart. "Do you remember last year when Ms. Robb talked about your freckles? Remember when the kids teased you by calling you fat? Sugar, people have their own views about every situation; that doesn't make it right, and it doesn't make it fair. Sometimes their remarks are not very loving, but they are *their* opinions, just as you have *your* own opinions that others may not like."

Grandmother began to laugh. "I *like* your elephant, and you like it; that is all that matters."

Grandmother's words were like sweet homemade vanilla

ice cream—cool and inviting—so tasty you wanted to take in every drop of its heavenly elixir.

The words of my Champion turned around the tears of a little girl lost in defeat, wrapped in depression, and swaddled in shame.

Extending her large arms, she pulled my small body into her extra-large breasts. I placed my arms around the front portion of her stomach and used her breast as a soft pillow. Resting my head, I awaited the love hug that she always gave me in times like this.

"Let's go make dinner," Grandmother said, as we made our way towards the kitchen.

* * *

The next day at school, Ms. Robb seemed to be in a really bad mood. During our class reading session, she interrupted MiJean Scott. "Wait a minute, wait a minute," she demanded. The reading session came to a halt.

"Those gardeners are always making that foolish, dang noise. I am so sick of it!" She slammed her reader on top of the desk and walked over to a nearby window. She unlocked and opened it. In a loud and aggressive voice, she began yelling at the gardeners, "Stop making so much noise!" An instant later, Ms. Robb closed the window, picked up her reader, and demanded that MiJean resume where she left off.

My mind was in another place. The story that involved Dick and Jane (The Older Years) was not interesting to me. I was only attracted to the pictures shown in the book. A large white house with all types of colorful flowers drew my attention from the class assignment. I loved turning the pages and looking at the art.

Suddenly, the classroom door opened and a woman of large stature walked into the room. It was Grandmother. She was dressed in her best Sunday go-to-meeting outfit: her best hat, white gloves, purse, and purple suit. She was so beautiful. Soulfully, she walked into the classroom with an aura of defined grace and dignity – old-school. That was my grandmother. I was not aware she would be coming to the school that day.

Ms. Robb was surprised, as well. "Good-morning, Ms. Gladys," our teacher's cheesy greeting began. "Welcome to our class." Grandmother merely nodded her head. Ms. Robb began the general dissertation she had prepared for all the visiting parents.

"That's fine," my grandmother interrupted. Sporting a puzzled look on her face, Ms. Robb stopped talking. Grandmother began to speak again.

"Did you tell Gladys that if she made the changes you suggested, her elephant would surely be included on the class mural?" Unfolding her arms, Grandmother reached inside her purse and pulled out my wrinkled picture of the elephant. She held the paper carefully in her white gloves.

Ms. Robb was completely thrown off guard. She had forgotten about the hurtful things she had shouted at me the previous day.

"Is this the elephant my granddaughter drew?" Looking closely at the picture, Ms. Robb nodded her head. "Good. I'm sure that such an honorable, intelligent, educated teacher such as yourself will keep her word. Gladys Jean made the changes you suggested, so the elephant *will* be present on the mural."

"Yes, uh, yes, definitely," Ms. Robb agreed.

"Have a good day," Grandmother uttered briskly. In one quick turn, she made her way towards the classroom door, never even acknowledging me.

Days later, my large, beautiful elephant was the central focus point in our class mural, and we won the third-grade class ribbon.

In retrospect, I certainly can see why members of our community often came seeking grandmother's wisdom and advice.

I certainly felt like a special child to have her as my "Elephant Champion."

Gladys Unimuke Wilburn has been quilting, drawing, and telling her folk-art stories for twenty years. Her *Harlem Hill Chronicles*, available on lulu.com, take place during the Jim Crow Segregation era in Fort Worth, Texas. Woven with the dream of youthful confidence, guarded in the hopes of family love, and fortified in the eyes of cultural history, Gladys takes the reader on a sneak peek journey into the life of one strong-minded young girl.

THE GREAT ESCAPE

KAREN A. PHILLIPS

L ush fields of open grassland surrounded the bare dirt enclosure where two friends focused on the task at hand. Shadows lengthened as the sun sank lower in the West.

"What's taking so long?" Duke's shoulders screamed in pain under the weight of his friend, Billy. He leaned against the cold metal bars. *Stay strong!* He had dreamt of this day for as long as he could remember. He wanted freedom so bad he could taste it. In his mind freedom was a juicy red apple hanging just out of reach. It took a while to convince Billy they could do it. After weeks of practice the two were able to position themselves where they could reach the mechanism that kept them caged. Duke would endure the burden of Billy upon his back. He needed his nimble friend to open the gate and release them from confinement.

Metal clanked and jangled as Billy kept at it. "I'm doing the best I can."

Their prison was once home to many more inmates. Only the two of them remained.

"I don't want to end up like our friends," Duke said.

Billy sighed. "You don't need to remind me."

"I keep reliving the day the Man killed Scout."

Billy stopped what he was doing as the memory returned like a bad nightmare. He could still hear the sound of the gunshot.

Duke groaned. "Hurry! I don't know how much longer I can last."

"It would help if you'd stop moving *and* stop talking. The Man might hear us."

Duke didn't care if the Man heard them. They had a language all their own the Man couldn't decipher. Duke locked his knees and stood still as stone. Sweat trickled down his nose and between his shoulder blades. He gritted his teeth. *How much longer?*

"Almost there," said Billy as if reading his friend's mind.

Bang! A door slammed shut and the Man with his Rottweiler headed in their direction.

"Too late! Here he comes!" Billy jumped from Duke's back and they did their best to act normal.

The Man entered the yard while the Rottweiler stayed outside. The dog sat on her haunches and stared. One white fang gleamed where a corner of her lip curled up. The Man went about his daily routine, inspecting the facility, while the dog patrolled the perimeter. When finished the Man surveyed the area, and, satisfied all was well, secured the gate. He whistled to the dog. "Let's go, Missy." The Man gave Duke and Billy a stern look. "You two behave yourselves while I'm gone." He waggled a finger. "No shenanigans." He laughed at his joke then strode off with the Rottweiler in tow.

They both disappeared behind the main building. An engine started, and the two friends watched through the bars of the gate as a truck rumbled onto the main road and vanished over the crest of the eastern hillock.

* * *

Duke wiped sweat from his face. "That was close."

"You're telling me," said Billy. "I hate to think what might've happened if we got caught."

"Confine us to a smaller pen, for sure."

"If Missy didn't tear us to shreds first," Duke said.

The once blue sky was now ablaze in ochre and crimson.

"Let's get back to it," Billy said. "Pretty soon it'll be too dark to see what I'm doing."

His words spurred Duke into action. He knelt at the gate and Billy once more climbed onto his back. This time Billy was able to slide the bar completely out of the holder.

"Success!" Billy hopped to the ground.

Duke pushed the gate open and they both rushed out.

"I can't believe we did it! We're free!"

They kicked up their heels, giddy with excitement.

* * *

Miles of open fields without fences stretched before them. They could get water from the creeks and hide out among the trees. They could live day-to-day on their own terms.

The sunset had died as if nature flung a tarp over her brilliant work of art, turning the terrain into an eerie palette of grey, where the unknown hid in the shadows. An owl hooted.

Duke stepped forward then turned to Billy. "Well, what're we waitin' for? Let's go!"

Just then a coyote howled, a desperate sound that underscored the bleak landscape.

Billy remained still and listened.

Duke shifted his feet, unsure now.

A wind picked up bringing a chill with it.

Duke shivered. "Hey, Billy. What if the neighbor's dogs are running loose out there?"

"The Great Dane and the Pitbull?"

"Yeah. Missy is bad enough but I hate to think what those two—" Duke couldn't finish.

Billy looked back at the empty yard. "Maybe it wasn't so bad after all."

"Regular meals."

"A roof over our heads."

Billy, the pygmy goat, looked his friend in the eyes. "The Man shot Scout because he was dying from equine colic."

Duke, the miniature horse, shuddered from the mere mention of the dreaded intestinal plight.

"He did the right thing, you know. He didn't want Scout to suffer."

Duke hung his head. "I know."

Billy made his way back to the paddock. His friend followed and together they closed the gate.

Duke took a deep drink from the water trough then exhaled as the adrenalin rush from their adventure subsided. "Feels good to be home."

Billy gave his friend a head-butt then motioned to the barn. "I don't know about you, but I'm exhausted. Let's hit the hay."

Karen A. Phillips lives in Granite Bay where she enjoys writing mysteries, MG/YA fantasy, and poetry. She has two short stories published: *Bad News is Good News* in the 2013 The Best of Capitol Crimes Mystery Anthology and *It's Written in The Stars* in the 2017 Capitol Crimes Anthology. She is also a published author of non-fiction articles such as *Vetting the Tevis – A brief history of the use of Veterinarians for the Western States Trail Ride.* She is a member of Sisters in Crime and Northern California Publishers & Authors.

HAROLD'S SEARCH

BARBARA BARRETT

Harold woke up hungry, and even yellow and brown grass sounded good. It was barely light among the tall rocks. The streak of gold that flashed as he hopped along the sandy trail startled him and he went to investigate. Always looking for new paths, he followed the light. Sometimes when the track curved right or left, he lost it for a short distance. His stomach was still growling, but his curiosity led him on. Several twists and turns later, the path ended and Harold scampered into the open air.

The valley below was small and sheltered from the hot, climbing sun by tall cliffs. There were patches of green grass just like home. Best of all, he saw abundant clumps of colorful flowers, some he had never tasted before. After the episode with the tall leafless tree with the sharp points, Harold was more careful.

He began with the nearest shrub and worked his way toward a small, fragile flower. Still hungry, he was about to eat it too.

"Please, don't eat me."

A flower that talked! Wait until he told his folks about this. Then he remembered he may never see them again. Tears rolled down his white cheeks.

"Why are you crying?"

"You did talk!" Harold was startled out of his tears.

"Of course, haven't you ever heard a flower talk?"

"No!"

"Well, maybe you never listened."

Harold admitted this was probably true. "Do you have a name?" Not knowing whether flowers did or didn't.

"Jenny." She fluttered her petals. "What's yours?"

"I'm Harold. I think you're the most beautiful flower I've ever seen."

Jenny's yellow deepened to gold. "Have you seen many flowers?"

"Oh, lots and lots, some of them a long way from here."

Jenny sighed, "I've always wanted to travel."

They talked all day, mostly about his adventures. Jenny couldn't hear enough. "I love this ground, Harold. It nourishes me, but it also holds me down and confines me. I envy you. Tell me about your home again. It sounds so beautiful. Like stories I heard when I was just a bud."

He told her about his family, his friend Sydney, and the game of hide and seek that brought him here.

Harold saw Jenny's puzzled look, "One player who is 'it,' counts while the others hide. Then the 'it' player searches and the game is over when everyone's caught or someone else is 'it'."

Jenny clapped her leaves. "What fun!"

"None of us ever caught Syd. I was 'it' and the only place I hadn't looked was across the river. It was forbidden but I went anyway. There were so many rocks, I finally admitted Sydney had won again. When I turned around, I thought I heard the river far off to my left. I didn't recognize anything and the more I walked, the more lost I became."

Harold shuffled his feet and hung his head, "I panicked and just ran until a shadow moved between me and the setting sun. I dodged and did everything I was taught. As I scampered between the rocks, I could feel him close to me. I was tired and it hurt to breathe. I thought I was a goner until I saw a small crack between two large rocks and ran into the hole just as the shadow leaped."

"And you never found your family or friends?"

Harold shook his head. "When I awoke, everything was brown. I just wanted to get back home where everything was green. For a long time, I searched a different direction every day and came back to the cave to sleep. It was safe and had the only water."

"The day I gave up hope of seeing my home, I sat in a dark corner all day. I would have stayed there forever, but I knew there *must* be someone else who was just as lonesome and might give up, if I did. It cheered me and I began to search for a friend, someone to talk with."

Jenny nodded. Her eyes sparkled with tears. "I'm also alone." She pointed a petal toward the wall of the nearby rock. He could see tangles of dead leaves and stems.

Harold saw Jenny every day after that, and if he was her eyes and feet, she was his heart. When he encountered death for the first time, she eased the pain. It was one of the tiny mice near Jenny's rock. For weeks she and Harold were speculating as each mouse scurried across the ground. One afternoon, the answer was revealed. Her neighbors were new parents and struggling to keep the young ones fed. Harold and Jenny watched the babies run and play. Nothing was too big or small to escape their attention. Keeping them out of trouble took both parents, and sometimes Harold, too.

This morning Harold heard them calling their mother. It was Harold who found her. She wasn't as fortunate, when the coyote chased her. Harold could still smell their enemy in the air. Bravely, mother mouse had led the danger away from her nest and the others were safe.

Blinded by tears, Harold covered her with earth and small stones. After he told her family, he went straight to Jenny.

"Why, Jenny? Why her? She never hurt anyone." Harold pounded his foot on the ground, until it hurt.

Silent tears ran down Jenny's face as she watched him. Tears for her own pain as well as his. Softly she touched him with one of her leaves.

Hours later when Harold finally spoke again, the anger was gone.

"Why, Jenny?"

"I don't know Harold. I've asked myself that many times," she told him gently.

"Did you ever find an answer? Did you ever find a way

41

to live with it?"

Jenny stared at the rock in front of her without seeing it. After a long pause, "I guess it's because I believe in the Promise of Spring. There is both pain and joy in the world, spring and winter. One brings death, and later, the other brings life. They go together, give one another meaning. Harold, those children, you and I and everyone, will go on living. We can mourn her and still be happy the rest of her family is alive."

"If there is no joy left, then death has taken us, too. She did what needed to be done and has gone on. Now it is our turn. We must face the days to come and a life without her. If not, we become dead ourselves. Before death, time is our enemy. Afterwards, it becomes a friend because it brings the Promise of Spring."

"It hurts so much, Jenny."

"I know, Harold," whispered Jenny because she couldn't trust her voice.

Harold heard the break that wasn't there. "I'm sorry, Jenny. Of course, you do. I'd forgotten about your parents."

When Jenny heard the gentle understanding, the dam broke. This time he comforted her.

*　　*　　*

"Wake up, Jenny, and look at this."

She opened her eyes at the sound of his voice. He'd been spending more time with her since the death of their friend.

"Harold, what are you doing here so early? The sun isn't even up."

"I know, but I've got to show you this. It's something I discovered last night. I could hardly believe it." With his paw, Harold began to make designs in the ground, stopping only to remove any small rocks or brush. For several minutes he was busy while she watched. Finally, he stepped back. "There, Jenny, see?"

She stared at it. "Well, I see the inside is round but what are those things all around it?" She turned her head from side to side. "I give up. What is it?"

"It's you!" Harold could barely stand still in his excitement. "The whole thing is you."

"Me?" Jenny looked at it again.

"Yup. Remember whenever I came back from exploring, I tried to describe what I saw? I mean, sometimes it was pretty hard but now I can show you. I can make all sorts of things on this ground." He looked at the sand with love for the first time.

Jenny clapped her leaves in delight. "That's wonderful." She looked back at the drawing with new interest. "Is that what I really look like?"

"Well, you're much prettier but it does give you an idea."

Her color deepened. "I think it's wonderful. Do another one, please."

Harold shook his head and with a mischievous grin went behind a nearby rock. He brought out a long, thin stick and handed it to her.

"It's your turn."

Jenny's eyes lit up as she clutched it between her leaves and bent over the ground.

All day they laughed and tried to stump each other. Whenever he wasn't there, Jenny looked for something he might miss. She no longer felt confined. It was wonderful to be able to take an active part in life.

* * *

Jenny looked down at the stones beneath her. It was early and the valley was quiet. She loved this time of morning because as the sun rose, the stones sparkled like the stars in the night sky. They were a gift from Harold. The green ones were the color of his eyes. Her own were filled with tears and with great effort she raised her head when she heard him coming. She dreaded his visit today.

43

"Hey, Jenny, I've got another pretty stone for you. This one is almost your color." Harold held it out for her to see and dropped it when he saw her limp petals and the stem that didn't stand quite so straight today.

"What's wrong? What is it?"

She raised her head a little and showed him the brown spot on her leaf.

He knew what it meant. Time was almost up for her, and spring was barely over. With no shelter, she wouldn't last long. Harold glared up at the sun and pounded his foot. He went close to Jenny and sat down. Neither spoke for a long time.

"I've got it!" Harold jumped up. "What if I sit over you during the hottest hours. I could even bring you water from the pool in my cave." He looked around. "There must be something I can use to carry it."

It took him awhile to find a small rock shaped deep enough to hold water. "There. See, Jenny? There's nothing to worry about."

Much to his surprise, Jenny began to cry.

"What's the matter?" Harold was bewildered. "Don't you like the idea."

"I like it fine. I'm just so happy," and to prove it she kissed him on the cheek.

His paw went to his face. Harold's eyes opened wide and his little bunny nose darkened to a deep rose. He stepped back, stumbled, got up and stumbled again. Jenny began to laugh. "Didn't *you* like it?"

Harold stood still; his legs didn't seem to work. "Yeah, I did. I guess I was so shocked. Well, nobody's ever . . . well, I mean my mother did, but nobody else ever . . ." He looked around frantically. "Maybe I'd better get some water right away." Harold grabbed the stone and ran. Just before he went over the hill, he glanced back. Jenny was still watching him. He threw her a kiss of his own.

Harold became Jenny's protection. During the day he sheltered her from the hot sun. In the evenings, he ate berries, fruits or nuts from the nearby bushes or trees. He no longer ate plants or shrubs.

With the water and sun protection, Jenny grew taller and lovelier each day.

"How come I've never seen a flower like you before?"

"We normally don't grow here."

Harold looked up from his watering. "Where do you come from?"

"Far away," she answered.

"What do you mean 'far away'," he asked. "Haven't you been here all your life?"

"Yes."

"Well, then . . ." Harold caught the laughter in her eyes. "Okay, give me the story."

"Well, it's a land very much like your own. My mama used to tell me such stories about it." Words tumbled from Jenny in her excitement. "Harold, it's across a great body of water and it took longer to get here than . . ." She searched for words, "than we've known each other."

"Come on, that would be forever," teased Harold.

Jenny blushed and protested. "No, it's true. I swear!"

"England," said a deep, unfamiliar voice.

A startled Jenny and Harold turned toward the sound.

The tall, leafless tree with sharp points went on, "It was England, my dear girl. That's where your parents were from."

Harold could only stare. Jenny, mindful of her manners said, "Permit me to introduce myself, I'm Jenny and this is my friend, Harold."

"I'm very pleased to meet you. My name is Sir Cedric Cactus."

"Why haven't you spoken sooner?" blurted out Harold.

"I didn't have anything to say."

"Mr. Cactus, did my parents really come from England?"

"Call me Sir Cedric. Yes, they did, and so did most of the plants here. I was tiny then, barely a tip above ground when they arrived."

"But how did they manage to move around?"

45

"They came with the Master and Mistress who lived over there." One of the flowers atop Sir Cedric's tall trunk tilted in the direction of the stone ruins close by. "Of course, they moved as easily as you, Harold, although I do remember thinking how oddly they were put together. No roots. The plants traveled in special containers. It was a long trip. Several flowers spoke of the dark and damp." He shuddered. "Unfortunately, only a few are left now."

Sir Cedric's voice softened, "Jenny, you were her favorite. She loved daisies best. Always said they reminded her of home."

"I'm the only one who remembers now. When they came here, the Master and Mistress gathered stones and wood and built their home. Every evening just after the sun set, they sat over there." Sir Cedric indicated the small shelter, surrounded on three sides by boulders, where Jenny stood. "Sometimes the Master would speak beautiful words to her:

"How do I love thee? Let me count the ways.

"I love thee to the depth and breadth and height my soul can reach.

"Of course, it's been a long time and I'm not sure of the words anymore," he apologized.

"But, it's lovely," breathed Jenny. She stole a look at Harold and their eyes met briefly.

"Every day the Mistress brought precious water and spoke loving words to us while the Master worked with a skinny stick on something flat and white. He was very weak and coughed a lot. At night while he slept, she came here and cried. 'Please God, cure him. Let him live,' I heard her whisper over and over."

"Then one day I saw her looking lovelier and happier. Right there, in their special place, she told him they were going to have a little one. It brought tears to all eyes to see the color come to his pale cheeks and watch him hug and kiss her."

Sir Cedric's voice broke. "All of us were so happy for them as they made plans."

By this time, every living thing in the valley was listening. He gave a deep sigh and continued. "She no longer wept at night. In fact, she hummed delightful little tunes most of the day." Sir Cedric cleared his throat and in a deep voice sang: "Lullaby and goodnight, thy mother's delight."[1] He hummed a few bars and finished with: "Lay ye down now, and rest, "May thy slumber be blessed! "Lay ye down now, and rest, "May thy slu....um....um....ber be blessed. "I don't think that's how it goes." Sir Cedric paused and shook his head.

"As the days passed, the Master grew stronger. His step was lighter and he walked faster, with more enthusiasm." Sir Cedric spoke in almost a whisper. There was no sound except his voice. Even the wind was quiet. "One night I heard strange sounds. She was moaning and he was running here and there carrying water. Towards daylight, he came out alone and walked slowly to their special place. He wept and wept. We tried to comfort him but he couldn't hear us. Finally, he collapsed from exhaustion.

"That evening, just before sunset, he buried her and the little one between the two big rocks behind you, Jenny. He covered them with daisies. For days he sat there, just staring. I mean, it had been terrible to hear him weep, but the silence was even worse. All of us were relieved when he finally went back into his dwelling. He needed food and rest. How could we know?

"Not long after, a loud noise echoed through the valley. Sometime later a friend came by and put him in the ground near his family."

Harold heard Jenny's quiet sobs. There were tears in his eyes and he looked quickly to see if anyone noticed. He needn't have worried. No one had dry eyes.

That night, strains of "lullaby and goodnight" could be

[1] Johannes Brahms, *Cradle Song* Op. 49, No. 4, 1868

heard as mothers sang to their own children.

Peace came to the small valley. Of course, some put on airs about their ancestors and got snobbish but for most, their common background became an excuse to talk with one another.

Thanks to Henry Cactus, a relative of Sir Cedric, Harold stayed in the valley each night. Henry was a plant of formidable width with a clear space inside his thorny limbs. Once Harold knew which branch to lift, he only went back to his cave for water.

Sometimes at night, he thought about that lonely night he almost gave up. If he hadn't kept searching, he wouldn't have found this valley or these friends. He wouldn't have found Jenny to talk and laugh with.

Barbara Barrett is an author and published poet who loves and appreciates words. Her essays have appeared on blogs, websites and in fanzines. Most recently, the *Suddenly Senior* website has published two articles: *Exploring Inner Space*, detailing her sensory deprivation tank experiences in search of self-awareness and limits of the mind; and *The Socratic Method and Other Tortures*, an amusing look at her law school years.

Barbara's *The Wordbook: An Index Guide to the Poetry of Robert E. Howard* (2009,) and several of her essays have received awards from the Robert E. Howard Foundation.

Member of Elk Grove Senior Center Writers Group; Elk Grove Writers Guild; and new member of Northern California Publishers and Authors, plus she has completed Gini Grossenbacher's eight week writing class, "Wired for Story."

Barbara lives in Galt, California where she is compiling a book of fiction and poetry. She can be reached at barbara_barrett@sbcglobal.net.

A DIFFERENT KIND OF CHRISTMAS

CHARLENE JOHNSON

"Are you sure you want to go through with this?" Felicity Singleton asked as she hung an ornament on the Christmas tree.

"Of course," Dex Brooks replied, handing her another ornament. "I already told my mother your family is coming. She's looking forward to meeting them. And she really wants to meet you too."

Felicity grimaced, knowing it was too late to change their plans. They had discussed it weeks ago. Her concern was her family. They were not shapeshifters and would be horrified if they found out that she was. They would never understand.

How could she begin to explain the freedom being a shapeshifter gave her? A freedom she now shared with Dex. The two of them, running through the forest in fox-form, made her feel whole. It was something she could never share with her family.

She hadn't seen her family in years, but Dex had encouraged her to reach out to them, and she did. It brought tears to her eyes when she remembered the sound of her mother crying on the phone. Her father was equally happy to hear from her. Only her brother was angry with her for not staying in touch. He slowly came around after a few long midnight phone calls. Her relationship with her family was getting back on course and she was thankful.

It wasn't her family's fault they became estranged; it was hers. She was afraid she would shift one day and one of them would see her. That's why she moved so far away from upstate New York. After talking to them, she realized how much she missed them. Maybe her family spending the holidays with Dex's family wouldn't be so bad. Then again, there was the shapeshifter thing.

In the months she and Dex had spent together, she grew to know what a kind, loving man he was. But that really started when he rescued her after the hunter shot and nearly killed her while she was in her white owl form. If not for him, she would have died in the forest. He nursed her back to health, and reluctantly was going to let her go. But she'd grown to care too much about him to let him send her away. Before he could do that, she revealed herself to him. It was the best decision she ever made.

"I can't wait to meet your family, Dex. I'm a little nervous about mine, though. What if they see one of you shift? How do we explain that?"

Dex took her hand and kissed it. "I'll make sure my family understands. I promise they will be on their best behavior. Even my rambunctious, impulsive twin brothers."

Felicity smiled as her heart turned over with love. "After some of the stories you told me, I'm scared of them."

"I can't blame you. My mother used to say she didn't know how she lived through raising them. They were always messing with the neighborhood kids. I can't tell you how many times the neighbors came over to warn us about the mountain lion their kids saw running down our street. My mom and dad knew it was one of my brothers."

Felicity put her arms around his neck. "I trust you. I have since the moment you saved me."

"You saved me first," he replied as he pulled her close. He was so glad he had found her. Rescuing her, even before he knew what she was, brought him back to life and gave him purpose. He'd been drifting for so long. Being with Felicity made him believe in the impossible.

"I thought we could leave early in the morning. It's a twelve-hour drive to Lake Crescent. We should get there by six in the evening."

"Sounds good to me. I'd better go pack."

*   *   *

The drive to Dex's parents' custom-built log cabin was uneventful. The traffic was minimal since they left in the middle of the week. Christmas was on a Monday, so traffic wouldn't get bad until the weekend.

Dex glanced over at Felicity. She was a beautiful statue, rigid and quiet. He wondered if she worried about meeting his parents or how the long holiday weekend would play out. Once they got settled, he would suggest a run in the forest.

"Felicity, you've been quiet for hours. Are you okay?"

She turned to him. "Yes. I'm a little nervous about meeting your parents."

"Why? You talked to my mother on the phone."

"I know, but meeting face to face makes it real."

"I hope you know that whether my family likes you or not doesn't matter to me. But you don't have to worry. They'll love you. I've never brought anyone home for the holidays. My mom is thrilled. My dad is a pushover and my brothers, well," he paused, "they will be infatuated with you, for sure. How can they not? You are beautiful inside and out. They will all love you."

Dex pulled into the long driveway and cut the engine. He took Felicity's hand. "Are you ready?"

Felicity swallowed hard. "Yes," she said with trepidation.

They got out of the car and walked onto the wraparound front porch. Before Dex could turn the doorknob, the door flew open. An older woman beamed at them.

"Dex, sweetie, I'm so glad you made it!" Emma Brooks exclaimed and hugged her son. "How was the drive?"

"Not bad." He pulled Felicity forward. "Mom, this is Felicity."

His mom smiled and hugged her. "It's so good to finally meet you."

Felicity smiled back. "Likewise." She looked around. "You have a lovely home."

"Thank you, dear. We love it here. With the forest in our

backyard, it's convenient, too." Dex's mom winked. She took Felicity's arm. "Come, I'll introduce you to the others while Dex gets your luggage out of the car."

Felicity walked with Dex's mother to the family room. Dex's father, Ben, was sitting in a brown leather recliner, and his younger twin brothers sprawled on the large couch like two bookends. They were watching *Man VS Wild*.

"Bear is going the wrong direction," one of the brothers shouted.

"No, he's not," the other one argued. "It's a stinking TV show; he can't get lost."

"Please, he's a human. You know they don't have a good sense of direction."

"I don't know why you like this show so much," the twin with sandy blonde hair complained.

"Bite me," the dark-haired twin shot back. "You make me suffer through *Dancing with the Stars* every Monday."

"Boys," Dex's father growled. "We have company." He stood up and walked toward Felicity and his wife.

"Dex and Felicity just arrived," Dex's mother announced.

His father smiled. "Felicity, a pleasure." He gestured to his sons. "This is Johnny and Joel."

The twins jumped off the couch and approached. "Very nice to meet you." In turn, they pulled her into a bear hug. Joel held onto her a little too long.

"Unhand my girlfriend," Dex ordered, as he entered the family room. "You two need to find a girlfriend of your own."

Joel grinned. "I couldn't help it, big brother. She is so beautiful and a shifter, too. How did you get so lucky?"

Dex grinned at her. "Right place at the right time."

"Do you have any sisters?" Johnny asked.

Felicity laughed despite her embarrassment. "I'm afraid not. I'm the only girl in my family."

"Too bad," the twins said in unison.

Dex looked at Felicity. "You got that right." He took her

hand. "Let's go for a run. I promised to show you the forest I grew up in."

Felicity smiled. "Sounds great. It will be good to stretch my legs after being in the car so long."

"Johnny and Joel, take Dex and Felicity's luggage to Dex's room," Emma ordered. "I'm going to finish dinner."

* * *

It felt good to be out in the woods after the long car ride. The white fox followed the red fox through the trees. Fall leaves covered the ground. The first snow had not yet fallen, but there was a distinct chill in the evening air signifying it would come soon. The sound of chirping birds and the rustle of leaves filled the air. They weren't alone. Life was all around them, and they were content.

The red fox walked into the clearing and sat on his hind legs, surveying the scenery before settling down to casually groom himself. The white fox hid behind the branches of a Red-osier dogwood, watching him. She quietly stalked her mate as if he were the prey, moving silently along the leaves, inch by inch.

The red fox knew what his mate was doing. It was a game they played. He was the prey this time. He continued to groom himself, ignoring the sound of her paws on the brittle, dry leaves. He knew she was getting close. Soon the fun would begin.

She pounced on him without warning. They rolled around on the leaves, playfully nipping at one another. The red fox escaped and glided through the trees, the white fox in quick pursuit. A black-tailed rabbit came into view, diverting their attention. They chased it with no intention of capturing it.

The rabbit sprinted under a snarled tangle of thick tree branches and disappeared. The foxes lost interest and began chasing each other. This time, the white fox was the prey. They frolicked in the forest until they were exhausted. They lay curled together on a tree limb to rest. Soon, they would have to return to their human forms. Dinner time was approaching, and it wouldn't do for them to be late.

*　*　*

They spent the next few days getting ready for Felicity's family to arrive. The cabin was abuzz with activity. Dex's mother wanted everything to be perfect. Felicity worried more about what would happen when they did arrive. Dex reassured her that everything would be fine.

The next day, Dex and Felicity took his dad's Ford Expedition and headed to SeaTac Airport to pick up her family. It was Christmas Eve and the traffic was heavy, but they still managed to make good time. Felicity was quiet for most of the two hours they were on the road.

"Everything all right, baby?" Dex asked.

She turned her head to him, her face serious. "I'm nervous is all. Talking to my family on the phone is far different than meeting face to face. How will they see me?"

"Your parents will see you as the daughter they've missed so much, and your brother will feel the same way too. You were worried about my family, but you didn't need to be. I told you everything would be fine."

Felicity smiled. "I love your family. And those brothers of yours. I bet there wasn't a dull moment growing up with them."

Dex laughed. "Not one."

Felicity's mother called her when they landed. The Singletons were waiting for them on the sidewalk by the time Dex pulled up to the curb in front of baggage claim.

Dex got out of the car and opened the rear hatch before joining Felicity and the Singletons. It was a wonderful, heartfelt reunion. Felicity, her parents and her brother, Bobby, embraced in a big group hug. Tears were flowing freely. He was elated to see the woman he loved so happy.

"You must be Dex," Carl Singleton said, holding out his hand.

Dex shook it. "It's very nice to meet you, Mr. Singleton."

"Call me Carl." He turned to his wife. "This is Mary, Felicity's mom."

Dex shook her hand. "I'm so glad you all could make it."

"How could we refuse?" Mary replied and put her arm through her daughter's. "I would have traveled anywhere to see my daughter."

"I'm Bobby," Felicity's brother said and shook Dex's hand.

"Felicity has told me so much about you."

Bobby rolled his eyes. "I can imagine what she told you. I assure you, none of it is true."

Felicity punched his arm playfully. "I only told him the good stuff."

"The really good, bad stuff," he asked wickedly, "or the good stuff?"

She laughed. "The good stuff, of course."

*   *   *

Christmas morning brought five inches of pristine snow. Felicity told Dex she wanted to go for a walk before she helped his mom fix an early Christmas dinner. Mary had volunteered to help, but Emma wouldn't hear of it, so Felicity's parents and Dex's father were in the family room watching *White Christmas* on TV. Bobby was on the front porch making a phone call. The twins had gone out earlier and hadn't come back yet.

The forest was magical. The sunlight shone brightly on the snow-covered trees and sparkled along each branch. The air was crisp and silent so early in the morning. They walked along the natural path and only stopped when a family of deer crossed in front of them.

"Things are going pretty well," Dex said as they walked along the path.

"Yes, they are. My family is having a great time. Thank

you so much for letting them come."

"It wasn't all me. It was my mom, too."

Felicity stopped to face him and linked his fingers with hers, her face serious. "Dex, since we met, you've taken care of me. I owe you so much."

"No, you don't. You brought meaning back into my life. I was lonely, and you revived me."

"I love you, Dex."

"I love you too."

*   *   *

A few hours later, Bobby burst through the kitchen door and slammed it behind him. He leaned against it; his chest heaving as he tried to catch his breath.

Emma and Felicity looked at him in surprise. Emma was putting rolls in the oven, and Felicity was peeling potatoes.

"What's wrong, Bobby?" Felicity asked as she laid down the knife and potato to focus on him, her eyes filled with concern.

"I saw three large gray wolves," he shouted. "One of them tried to attack me."

Carl and Mary came running from the family room as Ben followed slowly behind them, a smile on his face. He winked at his wife.

Felicity glanced at Emma. Dex's mother's lips twitched with a smile, but she quickly recovered. Felicity had to bite her lip not to smile, too. There was no doubt who the three wolves were. Dex had left her in the kitchen, and told her he was going out to see where the twins were.

She faced her brother and frowned. "Where, Bobby? Where did you see them?"

"Down by the lake. Three humongous gray wolves. I was walking along the path, heading to the dock, when I saw three wolves bound out of the woods to the water's edge. Two of them ignored my presence and went to drink. The third didn't. I looked at him, he looked at me and started growling."

"Did he approach you, dear?" Emma asked, her words filled with concern, but her eyes twinkling.

Bobby accepted a glass of water from his sister and took a large gulp. He spilled a little and wiped his mouth with the back of his hand. "He bared his teeth and stalked toward me, growling as he advanced. Suddenly, he stopped, sat down and began licking his paw."

"What did you do then?" Ben asked.

"I got the hell out of there before he changed his mind."

"The wolves probably already ate and needed water. He was playing with you. If he meant business, he would have attacked," Emma said and put the oven mitts on the counter. "The most important thing is you are safe."

"I agree," Mary said.

His father nodded. "This isn't the city, son. You have to be more careful."

"There are predators in the city, too," Bobby pointed out. "They just don't have claws and long, sharp fangs."

"True," his father acknowledged.

"At least in the forest, you know what a predator wants. Not so easy in the city," Ben added as he walked over to stand by his wife.

"Wolves usually don't come out until dusk to hunt," Emma said.

"Be glad they weren't hungry or things would have turned out much differently," Felicity told him. "Dex said wolves normally hunt in packs. It's better not to be wandering too far away, little brother."

Bobby smiled, sheepishly. "I guess you're right. I didn't think about it."

Felicity turned away and busied herself by picking up an oven mitt and opened the bottom oven door to check the ham. If she looked at her brother now, she would lose it. She was sure she knew who her brother saw by the lake.

Dex, Joel, and Johnny came in the kitchen door, looking around at the gathering. "What's going on?" Dex asked.

"Bobby saw gray wolves by the lake," his mother replied.

"Really? We just came by there. We took a run in the woods. I didn't see anything except some ducks." He looked at his brothers. "Did you guys see anything? You were ahead of me."

"No," Johnny and Joel answered in unison.

Dex frowned. "Are you sure they were wolves? The neighbors have a couple of rambunctious huskies who get out of their fenced-in yard every now and then. Perhaps that's what you saw."

"No," Bobby insisted. "It was wolves, three of them."

Felicity walked to her brother and nudged his shoulder. "Now that you are okay, why don't you go finish watching *White Christmas* with mom and dad?"

"We can watch *How the Grinch Stole Christmas* after it goes off," Johnny said.

"I love that movie," Joel replied.

"I do too," Bobby echoed and followed his parents and the twins into the family room.

Felicity gave Dex a conspiratorial nod and he smiled.

"Great idea. I'll be along in a few minutes to join you," Emma announced. "Dinner won't be ready for an hour."

Dex watched his brothers and their guests disappear into the family room. He looked at Felicity and his parents, and they all laughed quietly.

"You and your brothers will have to run deeper in the forest, especially when we have guests," Ben said in a low voice.

"I doubt Bobby will stray far from the house now that one of your brothers scared the life out of him," Mary added.

Dex chuckled. "I didn't realize he was out there. I thought he was inside with your folks."

"He was, but he got bored and said he was going outside to make a phone call," Felicity added.

Dex leaned down and kissed his mother's cheek. "We'll be more careful from now on."

* * *

After dinner, the Brooks and the Singletons sat in front of the Christmas tree to open presents. Dex watched them finish before he pulled the small red velvet box out of his jeans pocket.

"That's all the presents," his mother declared. "I hope everyone got what they wanted for Christmas."

"There's one more present, Mom," Dex said. "It's for Felicity."

Felicity gestured around her. "You've already given me enough, Dex."

He shook his head. "No, this one is the most important." He kneeled on one knee in front of her. He handed her the red velvet box.

Felicity looked at the box, then back at Dex's face. "What is this?" she asked, her heart beating wildly.

"Felicity, my love, you are my world. You mean so much to me. I can't imagine my life without you. Will you marry me?"

She opened the velvet box with trembling hands. Inside was a princess-cut diamond solitaire. "Dex, it's beautiful. I don't know what to say."

"Say yes," the twins said in unison as the others stared at them expectantly.

Dex and Felicity didn't notice. Their attention was focused on each other. There was no need for words. For a moment, the world around them stood still.

Tears formed in Felicity's eyes and she slowly smiled. "Of course, Dex, I'll marry you."

The room erupted in applause.

Dex stood up and pulled Felicity into his arms. "I was afraid you were going to say no," he whispered in her ear.

She stared into the eyes that captivated her white owl from the first time she saw him in the forest. Her beautiful red fox.

"Not a chance, Dex. This is forever."

Charlene lives in Sacramento, California. She is married and has a son, a daughter and four grandchildren. Books have always been her passion. She started reading at an early age and progressed to full-length books by age nine. The first book series she read was Dark Shadows.

She's writing two book series – Circle of the Red Scorpion and Sterling Wood. Charlene has published five books, two short stories and three poems.

Besides reading and writing, her other interests are photography, travel, music, movies, musicals and Elvis.

Her quote – "I've traveled the world, crossed galaxies, traveled through time and explored history on the pages of books."

Websites–https://www.circleoftheredscorpion.com & https://www.sterlingwoodseries.com

Email – circleoftheredscorpion@gmail.com

CAESAR ON THE THRONE

DUNCAN MACVEAN, D.V.M.

This fine potbellied pig was the monarch of the turf at the Land's house.

I was at the home to perform a physical examination and to update vaccinations for the Land family's privileged pet, who lived a cushy life in their regime. They were the first to admit to that. Subservient they were.

"Hi, I'm Dick and this is my wife, Betty. Come on in 'n meet our boy, Caesar." They led me through the living room, through a dining room, through the kitchen, and into a sunroom at the back of the house. This was Caesar's room.

Along the back wall was a bank of windows, too high for Caesar to see more than the overhang of the roof, sky, and the top limbs of a couple of trees. The wall was south-facing, so plenty of daylight streamed into his room; especially cozy in winter. A large electric fan stood in one corner of the room. No doubt there were plenty of cooling breezes in summer, since in addition to the standing fan, there was an overhead ceiling fan. To the left were two plastic bins containing dog toys, both rubber squeaky kinds and stuffed animals. Near the wall to the right was a huge dog bed with a rumpled heap of blankets over one side, trailing off onto the linoleum floor.

I commented, "Looks like Caesar sleeps in comfort, with all those blankets and the soft mattress." While raising my eyebrows in wonderment, I added, "Where did you find such an oversized dog bed?"

Betty answered with a prideful smile, "We had a small dog bed when we first got him twelve years ago. But he grew so big! I bought two of the largest dog beds I could find and sewed 'em together with leather strips. But he outgrew that.

What you see now is four large dog beds knitted into one."

Why not buy a large mattress? "But there are no ridges in the middle. How did you . . ."

Betty continued, "I simply slit the edges that were to come together, removed some of the stuffing, and stitched it back. Caesar sleeps like a baby."

A rather large baby. "Okay, nice job. Let's take a look at your baby."

"Probably out back." Dick pointed to the door in the left wall—a door that had the bottom half of it hinged to swing out like a heavy-duty double-wide doggy door. It was padded at the bottom, like weather stripping.

Dick led me out into what was euphemistically called a "backyard." The grass was sparse, clumped, with uneven patches of dirt, no doubt the result of indentations from Caesar's hooves and his rooting for worms or grubs. Flower beds along the fence were trampled.

No Caesar.

As we walked back inside Dick commented, "He's probably watching TV."

TV?

We marched through a hallway with well-worn flooring to a bedroom halfway down the corridor. Off on one side of the room was a low-slung overstuffed couch with an overstuffed pig stretched out on it. Caesar looked to be nearly a couple hundred pounds. His color was pale pink with small brown spots. He was quite attentively looking at the television set on the opposite side of the small room. There was a loveseat next to the couch.

Dick explained. "He's really smart. I think he knows what's happening on the programs he likes to watch. We set it to Animal Planet. If he grunts loudly, he wants us to change channels. So, we tune to Discovery or National Geographic. Other times he wants the music channels. He stares off into space as if in reverie whenever classical music is played. He doesn't care much for rock." Motioning toward the loveseat, Dick added, "We often join him for 'family time.' We used to sit with him, but he's gotten too big for us to join him on his couch. We use the loveseat."

"Such a life!" I said. "I can do some of the physical examination with him lying on the couch, but I'll need him to stand up for the rest of the exam."

I walked over to Caesar and held my hand out in front of his snout so he could get a good whiff of me. He barely sniffed. I spoke to him about needing his cooperation for the exam. He raised his snout in a way I interpreted as snooty and an "I can't be bothered" attitude, as if to say, "Do what you must, but don't interrupt my program."

Retrieving my stethoscope and otoscope/ophthalmoscope from my medical bag, I proceeded with the exam. I didn't bother to get out the rectal thermometer. *Surely he would object to that distraction.* Anyway, he checked out fine in all respects. A little tearing at the corner of the eyes, but no more than usual for an overweight pig. Fatty eyelids push eyelashes in to where they can scrape against the eyeball.

I inquired about feeding. The Lands' answers were the usual excess table scraps with "I know, I know. We spoil him." Their contriteness shortened my feeding regime lecture.

I reached in my satchel and took out a vitamin treat to lure Caesar up off the couch for the rest of the exam. He wouldn't budge. I tried nudging him. No go.

Yielding to his stubbornness, I said, "Okay, I'll try to palpate his internal organs from the sides of his belly." I knelt down with one knee on the couch and pushed on his abdomen. He didn't cooperate well, nudging my hands away from his side by pushing with his snout. *At least you're paying attention to me.*

Dick offered a solution. "He loves grapes. We'll get some from the freezer. Bet he gets up then."

Betty went off to the kitchen and returned holding a small aluminum bucket that contained a few frozen grapes. When she swung the container back and forth, the grapes made a rattling sound like marbles in a tin can. It worked. Caesar slowly rolled over the edge of the sofa and stood. He grunted, but didn't move any closer to the bucket.

"We need to bring the treats to him. He doesn't come to us. He actually prefers that we hand-feed him." She looked at me and moved her head back and forth. "I know, I know. He has us well trained."

"All right, then, you hand him one grape at a time, and I'll finish my exam while he stands here."

Betty held out a grape in the palm of her hand right up to Caesar's lips. He curled his lip, sucked the grape into his mouth and crunched it up. Betty proceeded this way with the next dozen or so grapes while I pushed up on Caesar's pendulous belly to palpate for any abnormalities. Everything was fine until I moved to his rear. There was a stringy object of some sort dangling from his anus. I grabbed hold of it and pulled.

Caesar bolted. I was left holding a wad of grass-like material stuck together with smelly stool. The Lands rolled with laughter. Caesar stood at the doorway glancing back at me with the unmistakable look of indignation and a snort that I heard as "How dare you?"

Caesar then ambled off down the hall.

Dick shouted, "Hurry up. Come on. You've got to see this," and went off along the hallway after his pig, leaving me holding the stringy, smelly mess.

Finding no convenient place to dump the load, I followed down the hall holding the green and brown clump in one hand, using the other hand to keep it from dripping onto the floor. I reached the room at the other end of the hall just in time to see Caesar walk up a wide wooden ramp from the floor to above the toilet to a wooden platform that had a hole cut out toward the back of it. Caesar reached the top, turned completely around, and faced me while he squatted and dumped a load down the hole. Standing full up, he wiggled his rear end a little, shaking off a last clump. Then he turned back around to the toilet tank and effectively pushed down the flush handle with his snout!

As calm as could be, he turned around and strolled down

the ramp with hips rolling as if he were a fashion model in a slow stately stride across a catwalk. With head aloof, he brushed by me as if I was not there and headed back down the hall toward the TV room.

While feeling a little humiliated holding the odorous prize in my hands, I also was impressed with Caesar's performance. I heard Dick say, "What did you think of that, huh? I built the ramp and trained him when he was young. Of course, I've had to keep enlarging and reinforcing the ramp and platform as he got larger."

I no doubt stimulated Caesar's need to go to the bathroom by tugging on that wad of stuff that dangled from his bum. Just like dogs, pigs will sometimes eat a clump of grass or weeds that end up passing all the way through.

Dick was grinning, half choking on a suppressed laugh. "You can drop that stuff in the wastebasket over there near the sink."

The basket was lined with a plastic grocery store bag. Easy disposal. I chatted with Dick while I squeezed soap out of a dispenser and washed my hands. "You did a good job with the toilet training. Pigs learn quickly. That is really clever. How did you get the idea? What was your training method?"

"I read in a pig magazine about some guy who built the same kind of toilet 'bowl' for his pig. I thought, 'Wow, what a great idea. I'm gonna do it.' I've done a little cabinetry on my job, so building it was not difficult. Training was easy once we discovered what reward worked best for him."

"Rewarding is the best. When he does what you want, you give him his reward treat. What was it?"

"Oreo cookies! He'll do anything for an Oreo. But we started using grapes, a healthier treat, once he got larger."

"Good. He's got the potty routine down well." I smiled. "He doesn't even have to go outside to relieve himself."

"Of course, we have our own toilet in the master bedroom. He stays out of there," Dick said with a chuckle. "There are a few other tricks we trained him to do, but now he's too old. Set in his ways."

I responded, "Maybe he is still capable of learning new ways, if he thinks it's in his best interests. Caesar seems like the type that will choose on his own what he wants to learn, now that you have established that he is king of his domain. He doesn't need to please you anymore. He pleases himself."

Dick nodded with enthusiasm. "Man, you can say that again! He's figured out how to push our buttons."

"He might just be ignoring you when you try new things now. Of course, grapes are not quite the incentive as Oreos, for sure. I'm not convinced 'you can't teach an old dog new tricks' applies to pigs. They're smarter than that. I know one guy that taught his old porcine companion to walk a labyrinth."

"You have a point there. He is the Emperor." Dick led me around with him to show me the front of the bathroom door. There hung a handwritten sign that read "Caesar's Throne."

Betty was still standing in the hallway. She added, "When he was young, he potty trained immediately. We taught him to sit, stay, fetch, and shake hands."

I smiled and said, with tongue in cheek, "Ha, I know some relatives of mine that aren't that smart!" We all laughed, nodding in agreement.

I asked them to lead me to a table with good lighting, so I could fill out the paperwork. We all went off to the kitchen, and I sat down at the dinette.

"Caesar's gait is excellent. No lameness, no swollen joints; and his hooves don't need trimming."

Dick then informed me, "Caesar does a good job of rubbing his hooves down himself. He digs in our backyard like a dog burying a bone."

"Ha, okay. His tusks don't protrude beyond his lips, so no need to cut the tusks. I don't see the need to boost his vaccines. You said earlier on the phone that he doesn't see other pigs or dogs (some canine vaccine-preventable illnesses can be transmitted to pigs). His breathing seems fine, and there is no snot on his nose like he might have if he had a respiratory problem. Unless he shows signs of illness, I don't think I need to see him again for another couple of years."

When we concluded our business Betty remarked, "Thank you, Dr. MacVean, for your kind assessment." With a chuckle she added, "And I'm sorry you ended up with a handful of poop."

A memorable visit to a crown monarch in his pigdom.

Duncan MacVean, D.V.M., Ph.D., was a professor of veterinary medicine at various universities and has published in peer-review journals. He also worked with wild animals in Southeast Asian jungles and as a consultant for the Malaysian National Zoo and The Brookfield Zoo in Chicago.

Dr. MacVean operated a house-call veterinary practice for the past 28 years in his hometown of Sacramento, California, He is now retired and lives in Placerville, CA. His memoir, *My Patients Like Treats: Tales from a House-Call Veterinarian*, was published in May 2018 by Skyhorse Publishing. His chapter, *Pigaro, Pigaro, Pigaro*, appears in the NCPA anthology *Birds of a Feather*.

ONE MORE STONE

DOROTHY RICE

I was 14 when we moved to Mill Valley, across the bay from San Francisco. This was in 1968, one-year post-Summer of Love. The family consisted of my parents, two sisters, and Nigel, a gawky, adolescent German Shepherd my college-age brother had left at the house and never come back for. Nigel hadn't mastered lifting his leg to pee—he never really would—and, when faced with a leash, he froze like a balky donkey. But he had a generous smile, wide toasted corn flake paws and a kinked tail, perpetually bent at a jaunty right angle. We blamed the dog's behavioral quirks on the psychedelic drugs my brother said he'd been fed as a puppy.

As kids, we'd only had fish, turtles and parakeets. My parents groused about Nigel at first, a lot, Dad with the most vehemence, which may have had more to do with resentment at my brother than anything the dog ever did. But Nigel stayed, and in a household where the golden rules were that children were best seen and not heard and if we didn't have something nice to say, we shouldn't say anything, Nigel became sounding board, pillow, footrest and refuge. I slipped him illicit treats from the kitchen, scratched the spots he couldn't reach, let him lie on the couch and whispered poetry into his pointy ears, comforted by the solemn depths of his liquid, brown eyes.

In return, I assumed Nigel would love me best. But it didn't work out that way. His allegiance was to my taciturn, grudging father. The dog followed Dad like a furry shadow. When he left for work, Nigel waited for his return, coming back to life when the Dodge van crunched into the driveway at day's end.

Dad was an art teacher in the San Francisco public schools. The rush hour commute across the Golden Gate meant he wasn't home a lot and even when he was, my father kept to his workroom beneath the house. With a sniff—so we'd know it bugged her—Mom would say he preferred his own company to ours. I suspected she was right. But at least my dad was productive. I believed there wasn't anything he couldn't create or fix.

After the move, it was months before I had any friends at the new high school. I spent lunch hours alone, on the sloped front lawn with a sketchpad on my canted knees, head bent in concentration, the breeze lifting my unruly hair— always more frizz than curl. I wasn't lonely. I was an artist in the throes of creativity. At least that's the impression I hoped I gave as I strained to catch the conversations of the chattering clumps of kids who passed me by.

After school, before my parents got home from work, I would sneak downstairs to study the sketches on Dad's desk, the finished paintings propped against the wall, whatever work-in-progress rested on the easel. I breathed in wood dust, paint and thinner, ran my fingers over the brushes and tubes of color, careful not to disturb the ordered clutter of his private world.

Like the dog, I waited for the sounds of Dad's return.

"Come on then," he would say, after he'd changed out of his work clothes and into a paint spattered t-shirt and slacks. And Nigel would race after him, collar jangling, out the front door and down the steep side of the house to the backyard for the requisite game of fetch-the-rock.

Nigel was a rock hound. We'd tried to interest him in balls or sticks. But he would ignore them and lay rocks at our feet, some of them boulders so large he struggled to drag them across the yard, whining and pawing at the earth, until one of us relented and tossed him a stone. In time, we accepted it as another of his idiosyncrasies.

In my bedroom under the peaked A-frame roof, I sat at

the drafting desk Dad had rescued from a school dumpster and refurbished for me. The smell of ground beef sizzling on the stove wafted up the stairs. One ear cocked to my open window, I put the finishing touches on a sketch I'd begun at lunch, a girl with a halo of wild Medusa hair, like mine only better, wilder. I added two crescents to the slender chest, squiggly circles for nipples. It was good, I thought, good enough to show my father.

His voice carried through the open window.

"Here you go, boy," he said. I pictured him picking up a rock, rolling it in his hand. "Just a few more stones. I've got work to do."

That was my cue. I tore my bare-breasted girl from the pad, thundered down the carpeted stairs and out the front door, the crisp white page fluttering at my side.

Our backyard consisted of a rectangular stretch of rocky, unplanted dirt that ran the length of the redwood house. Beyond that, the bushy hillside plummeted to a narrow road at the edge of our property. As I rounded the corner, Nigel came tearing up the hill and onto the rise, a plum-sized rock clamped in his jaw.

"Bring it here then, you great simpleton," Dad said. "Come on."

With the tip of his tail pointed towards the sky, Nigel trotted back to Dad, gums and tongue pink and dirt-flecked, the rock a jaw-breaker jutting from one side of his mouth. My father wrestled with him for the stone and tossed it again, aiming for the hillside, but Nigel leapt and in a feat of canine acrobatics, intercepted the speeding projectile mid-flight. Dad and I flinched in unison as it clinked against Nigel's teeth.

"Ye gads," my father said. "Don't swallow it."

My father reached for another rock from the loose pyramid at his feet and tossed it with an easy flick of his wrist. Nigel dropped the stone in his mouth and tore off after the new one, churning up dirt with his great cloddish paws. He plunged down the steep hillside and disappeared.

Hands at his waist, Dad straightened, stretching out his

back. He gazed out over Tamalpais Valley, the opposite side speckled with houses peeking through the trees, a blanket of downy white mist unfurling over the tops of the hills. My father would have been close to fifty then—younger than I am now. He was still lean and muscled, with wavy black hair, long enough over his ears and collar that my friends thought he was cool, for a dad.

"A million-dollar view, isn't it?" he said.

"Worth the price of admission," I said.

"The life of Riley," he said, with a wry chuckle.

My father was a font of stock phrases and truisms. Perhaps because he spoke so little, coming from him, these old chestnuts had the ring of profundity.

I still clutched my drawing, half hidden behind my back.

"What's that you've got there?" he said.

I handed him my drawing.

Dad held my sketch at arm's length, his expression inscrutable, eyes narrowed, the slightest upward turn at the corners of his mouth. Nigel reappeared, chuffing like a laboring engine.

"It's nothing. Just a silly doodle from school," I said, with a shrug.

"Mind if I keep it? To share with my students."

Cheeks flushed with pride, I studied the ground at my feet.

* * *

Several years later, when I was away at college, Mom left my father for a gregarious work colleague with a toothy grin. Then it was just Dad, my younger sister, and Nigel, in the Mill Valley house. The dog began to lose weight. He stopped chasing stones. The vet diagnosed stomach cancer. We speculated it was all the rocks in his gut.

"Poor, foolish creature," Dad said. "I tried to tell him."

He buried Nigel on the hill behind our house and planted a fruit tree to mark the grave.

*   *   *

Dad died five years ago at 92. Going through his belongings, my sisters and I emptied one of his closets, filled to bursting with paintings and half-finished canvasses.

At the back of the closet was a dusty portfolio, its cardboard covers warped from standing on edge so many years. We laid it flat on the carpet and removed the contents piece by piece, careful not to tear or smudge the delicate beige paper he'd used for sketches, the crinkly sheets of heavier white.

"This is different," my older sister said, squinting at a dappled watercolor, a riot of pastel wildflowers.

"It's mine," I said, reaching for it. "From my impressionistic phase. I can't believe he kept it." I made a face, mouth pulled down at the corners, chin crumpled like a bulldog's.

"You look just like Dad when you do that," my younger sister said.

Though it had been nearly 50 years, I remembered laboring over that piece in my bedroom at the top of the stairs, swirling a brush in a muddied tray of colors, hoping for a good one, good enough to take downstairs to my father, good enough to interrupt his Nigel time. Holding that watercolor in my hands, I was transported back to the rugged landing behind our house, the damp nip of evening in the air, Nigel thrashing his tail, every ounce of him intent on the dusty rock in my father's hand.

Dorothy Rice, a San Francisco native and long-time Sacramento resident, is the author of two published memoirs, *Gray Is the New Black* (Otis Books, June 2019) and *The Reluctant Artist* (Shanti Arts, 2015). Her personal essays and fiction have been widely published in journals and magazines, including *The Rumpus*, *Brain Child Magazine*, *The Saturday Evening Post*, *Hippocampus* and *Brevity*.

After raising five children and retiring from a career managing statewide environmental protection programs, Rice earned an MFA in Creative Writing from UC Riverside, Palm Desert, at 60. She now works for 916 Ink, a youth literacy nonprofit. You can find Dorothy at dorothyriceauthor.com, and on twitter at @dorothyrowena.

THE MACABRE MACAQUE

AMY ROGERS

How can you tell if you've frostbitten your backside? I'd been pondering this question for a good fifteen minutes when I realized that the numbness in my derriere pretty much matched my feelings for the boyfriend I was ice fishing with.

A gentle breeze of minus-ten-degrees ruffled the tips of my hair sticking out from a thoroughly inadequate polyester beanie. I laid my pole on the ice with the line still in the water. "I'm going back to the dorm."

Erik rubbed his hands. "Okay."

In that instant I knew it was over. Despite my best effort to fake it, I happen to like central heating and indoor plumbing. I would have to find a new boyfriend. A *better* muscular, blond, North-woodsy dreamboat. One who didn't mind walls, and who actually went to class.

This wasn't going to be an easy task.

I walked back to campus, lifting my knees high to fire up my thigh muscles for warmth. The sky was clear and the sun was cold and bright, a rare and welcome relief to the typical winter gray of Minnesota. I was prone to seasonal depression so I savored the light, as much as I could while shivering. I decided that without a boyfriend, I would need a job. A distraction to keep me from falling into a funk over this breakup. And with my social life moving indoors, I'd need money for bar tabs and tickets and all that.

So, the next day I marched into the student employment

office. The harried woman staffing the desk peered through her reading glasses. "I see you're majoring in psychology. I have a job with the anthropology department. That's close."

I didn't agree with her matchmaking logic, but whatever. I took the job. For five hours a week I cataloged finger bones. Seriously. They were mostly primate bones, sometimes human. I sorted, labeled, and filed them. This was not as creepy as it sounds. The bones were so clean and dry, you could imagine they were fake. Don't ask me where the department got them or what they did with them once I was finished. That was beyond my pay grade, and despite what Student Employment Lady says, psychologists don't care much about bone structure.

One slushy, miserable day, the professor stopped me on my way to the bone-sorting desk. "I need you to run an errand for me," she said. "They have something for us over at the med school."

I felt a tingle of suspicion. I'd heard macabre rumors of a project one of the graduate students was working on. "What is it?" I asked.

"A monkey. Macaque." She said it nonchalantly, as if this were the most ordinary thing in the world. My face must've betrayed my shock. "Not a *live* monkey," she said reassuringly. "It'll be wrapped."

She misunderstood my chagrin. A live monkey would've been fine. A dead monkey, whether wrapped, freeze-dried, or stuffed, was not something I wanted to be involved with. But a job is a job. I nodded. Transporting a packaged monkey couldn't be worse than gutting a fish, a useful skill I'd picked up from the ex-boyfriend.

I made my way across the sloppy campus and got admittance to a windowless basement in one of the medical buildings. After presenting my ID, I was given a grocery-type shopping cart with a large, unwieldy cargo wrapped in black plastic sheeting. I tried not to look at it too carefully.

As I pushed the thing off an elevator and through a loading dock door, I discovered it was surprisingly heavy. Outside, the sidewalk sloped upward. I leaned into the cart, shoving with all my might against the thick gray slush that grasped at the wheels. My feet slipped and I nearly fell.

A hand reached out to stabilize the cart. "Can I help you?"

I regained my footing and looked up. There stood a gorgeous hunk of a guy with a kind face. "Thanks," I said, regretting the shapeless overcoat I was wearing. While I didn't really need help pushing to the top of the rise, I definitely needed to know more about this man. I tried for a joke. "You come here often?"

"Whenever I need a shopping cart," he replied.

Witty. I liked that.

Together we reached the summit. I learned his name was Chaz, that he was a hockey player, and he liked margaritas on the rocks, no salt. While I'm a salt kind of girl, I figured this was not an insurmountable problem. I reached into my coat pocket for my phone so I could text him my number.

Apparently, he had the same idea. In a fateful moment of synchronicity, Chaz let go of the cart just as I did. Gravity took control. The cart teetered downhill, gaining speed, wobbling, and spraying slush in its wake. We both sprinted after it.

But we were too late. Going over the curb, the cart teetered and tipped. The formless plastic-wrapped mass toppled out and struck the pavement.

And a hairy arm with a wrinkled black hand popped out.

Chaz screamed. I screamed.

Chaz passed the fallen cart and kept running. And screaming.

I watched him swiftly disappear into a building. So much for Mr. Macho hockey-player. Can't handle a little monkey business.

I sighed. I would have to manhandle the primate back into the bag and cart on my own.

Until someone said, "Hey."

I turned toward that familiar monosyllabic voice. "Erik! What are you doing here?"

"Class," he said. Then without any comment or drama, he shoved that grotesque limb back into the bag. With the easy strength I remembered, he righted the cart. "You got this?"

I was about to dismiss him when it hit me. Erik was going to class, on a perfectly good ice fishing day. "I have to get it to the anthropology building. Would you mind?" I asked.

"Sure."

As we walked, he asked no questions. He just accepted me, and did what needed to be done. Maybe I wasn't bananas about him, but I decided to quit monkeying around with other guys.

"Cross country ski with me on Saturday?" I asked.

"Yep," he replied. "That'd be fun."

"More fun than a shopping cart of monkeys?"

"You betcha."

Amy Rogers, MD, PhD, is a Harvard-educated scientist, novelist, journalist, educator, critic, and publisher who specializes in all things science-y. Her thriller novels *Petroplague, Reversion,* and *The Han Agent* use real science and medicine to create plausible, frightening scenarios in the style of Michael Crichton. Formerly a microbiology professor at CSU-Sacramento, she is an Active member of International Thriller Writers, and serves as treasurer for Northern California Publishers and Authors. In addition, her local science journalism has been published in *Science in the Neighborhood*, and she runs the ScienceThrillers.com genre book review website. Amy lives in Sacramento with a herd of house cats and loves to get outside. Learn more at AmyRogers.com.

FRENCHIE – A LOVE STORY

CAROLYN RADMANOVICH

The day I was born, my mother whelped five other French Bulldog pups, along with me, Frenchie, the most handsome dog in the world. I know this because my mother informed me and she always told the truth. She'd sometimes enhance the facts, maybe, but never lie.

My days were filled with delight. I loved when my mother licked me so hard, I'd fall over. I would come back for more. Her big pink tongue would swipe right over my nose and mouth and I'd sneeze. She nuzzled and cuddled me. I would tussle and play with my brothers and sisters. Love surrounded me. I couldn't be happier.

As I grew, my mother told me someday humans would come and take me and my littermates away. My important job was to make my humans happy, give them affection, and protect them. I whimpered when she told me because I didn't want to leave her or my littermates.

Sure enough, one day a short, plump woman came to our house and picked up my sister and kissed her on the nose. "This is the one I want." My mother's master said, "Good choice," and they exchanged some pieces of paper and the woman took my sister away.

My mom's muzzle drooped, and she gave us extra attention that night. Life had been so blissful before this. Why did it have to change?

My mother told me that life was bittersweet, and I would be sad for a while when I was taken away. I wasn't to worry for I would find love and happiness again. I was doubtful, but my mother was wise and I listened.

The next day, I was told my new owner, Jacob, would

come to visit. When he arrived, he brought his wife, Susan. Jacob's eyes got big when he spotted me. He reached down and picked me up. "Ah, such a good-looking pup. I will call him Frenchie. He will be my birthday gift to you, Susan."

When Susan patted me on the head and scratched behind my ears, a funny fuzzy feeling grew in my belly. I surprised myself for I wasn't sad when she placed me in a box and put me in their car.

When we got to their home, Jacob carried me past the large lawn for running and playing on, and trees and bushes to pee on, and dirt to dig in. When I ran around in circles in the foyer, Susan laughed in delight to own such a playful and debonair dog as myself. She brought me puppy chow and boy did it taste good. What a relief to know she was such a marvelous cook.

When I finished eating, Jacob opened the door. Rex, their black Labrador retriever ran inside. He barked at me so I'd understand he was the boss. Such a monstrous dog, with those large canines. When he drew close, I put my head down and cowered. He then proceeded to lick me from one end to the other.

There were days when Rex and I would cuddle up and fall asleep together after prancing through the vineyards. He was my pal, but my true loves were my master and mistress, whom I adored.

Jacob would pull me onto his lap since my legs were too short to reach him. He'd then tell me what a great dog I was, and rub my belly and play with my long ears which he called "Dumbo" ears, whatever that meant.

After several happy months of being loved by my master and his wife, Rex asked if I had noticed that our master's wife was getting quite round about the middle and he suspected she would have a litter soon. I grew worried for now that I had found love once again, it might be snatched away from me by the new litter.

The next day, Rex found me with my head under my blankets, whimpering. He nudged me with his great black nose and asked, "Why are you so sad?"

"Because when the new litter arrives, our master and mistress will forget me. I'll no longer be their great dog. They won't hold me on their lap. Instead, they'll want to play with the new babies."

Rex barked at my ignorance and prodded me so hard I had to leave the privacy of my blankets. "If nothing else," he said, "we have our friendship. It's the purest love, where nothing is asked for and we simply enjoy giving."

I licked him across the nose. He was such a wise dog.

"Besides," Rex said, "life is good and bad, bitter and sweet, dark and light. Accept both sides and soon you'll find you've become more mature and accepting of the depth of existence."

A few weeks later, our mistress entered the house carrying two babies. "Ah, a small litter," I barked in relief. "I won't have so much competition."

Our mistress leaned down and let Rex and me sniff the babies. They smelled like milk and had an earthy muskiness about them. Rex and I licked the babies and she laughed. "I see you love them as much as I do."

As the days went by, Jacob and Susan spent most of their time doting on the babies. Our master still took us on walks in the evening, but made them shorter. The bounce in his step showed me he enjoyed his new litter and was happy. I still received pets and doggie snacks, but it wasn't the same. Jacob and Susan were splitting their love between Rex and me and the new litter. Perhaps they would give me and Rex away and keep the litter?

My life lost its spark. At least until the day my mother came to me in a dream. "You look sad, my darling pup."

I told her my concerns and she gave me advice on how to be happy. "Remember the moments of love, beauty, and silence within you. That way, even if you're surrounded by darkness, the light inside you will be so strong you'll not see the darkness."

"Yes, Mother. My wise mother. Anything else I need

to know?"

She licked my ears like she did when I was a puppy. "Yes, my precious whelp. When you are full of love, the whole world showers love. Whatever you put out will come back to you."

The dream faded, but not the words. They stayed with me.

One day, Rex and I sat guarding the baby carriage parked in the flower garden. Our master walked away for a few moments when his black, plastic box made a ringing sound. He talked into the machine and seemed distracted.

I saw the snake first. No one had to tell me it was evil, I just knew. The snake soundlessly glided over to the baby carriage and wound around the wheels and slithered upwards.

"The babies. I must help the babies!" I barked at the snake, but it didn't scare, so I pulled it off the buggy with my teeth. It reared around and tried to strike me, but I shook my head back and forth. The sound of the snake rattles buzzed in my ears.

Rex barked ferociously and our master finally looked over. He dropped his plastic box and rushed over with a stick and smashed the snake.

"What good dogs you are. You protected the babies. You'll get extra treats tonight and I promise to walk you more often. I realize I've been neglecting my great dogs." He patted us and then kissed the babies on the head.

When our master gave us our dog biscuits, I realized I hadn't been afraid when I bit the snake. I sensed I had to protect the babies. An ancient instinct had arisen in my chest. With my new wolf heart, I would protect my family today, tomorrow and forever, even if it meant risking my life. I was no longer a shy puppy. I felt assured of the love of my human family and of my best friend, Rex.

Fascinated by the wild west, Carolyn Radmanovich earned a history degree from San Jose State University. After a near drowning incident on the Russian River, she felt compelled to write her first book, *The Shape-Shifter's Wife*, about an anthropologist who time travels to the 1848 California gold rush and meets a handsome Frenchman.

The Shape-Shifter's Wife won the 2018 Independent Book Awards for Visionary Fiction. The sequel, *The Gypsy's Warning*, is Carolyn's current project. "Tex's Dream" was added to *Birds of a Feather, An NCPA Anthology*.

She won second place for the 2019 Memoir Contest for her short story, "Prod," with The California Writers Club, and participates in a Critique Group with the EGWA. Carolyn lives in Lincoln, California with her husband and cat, Tex. Her website is www.CarolynRadmanovich.com.

EACH TIME I DO

ELENA M. MACALUSO

I was four when my first cat died. "She died of cat fever," my mom told me. For years I pictured Tinkerbell, her body writhing and aching in pain under the grasp of a sweltering fever, wondering if the same could happen to me.

I was 12 when Samantha died of parvo. She was my brother's dog, but I loved her better than he ever could. I was the one who comforted her after my brother forcefully ejected her from his newly washed car. "Don't worry," I told her when I found her cowering in the garden. "I won't let him hurt you." I was too young to fully grasp the death of Tinkerbell; I was too young to fully grasp Tinkerbell. However, Samantha was a different story. I sobbed hysterically on my parents' bed on a hot June evening, my mother unable to soothe me. I felt like I was being severed in two, the pain so wrenching. Up until that point, I had never experienced such a profound loss.

I was 24 when Sabrina died. She was Samantha's sister, given to me by my brother shortly after Samantha died. Sabrina saw me through the turbulent (and sometimes lonely) teens and early adulthood. She had cancer, or something similar, and had been at the vet hospital for a few days when my parents made the decision it was "time." Sabrina wagged her tail when we went to her kennel to say goodbye. For a few moments, we all wondered if she was rallying. But like a terminally ill patient who provides loved ones with a few moments of lucid conversation before dying, Sabrina was not rallying; she was giving us one last hurrah. My mom stayed with her as the veterinarian administered whatever it is veterinarians administer when you put animals to sleep. My dad and I waited out by the car. I wept openly; my dad wept stoically. I went to work that afternoon.

Samson was technically my parents' dog. That didn't stop me from considering him every bit my dog. I'd "talk" to Samson when I called home to California from Kansas, where I was attending graduate school; I showered him with gifts on his birthday and Christmas; I took him to see Santa. Samson died four years after my dad died and was my mother's faithful companion as she learned to navigate widowhood. Samson's decline was prominently evidenced by his frequent inability to control his bowels, but Mom wavered back and forth for a month before deciding it was time to let him go. Finally, she scheduled him to be euthanized on a Thursday. ("I waited too long," she lamented afterward, up until her own death seven years later.) The night before, I slept in my childhood bedroom, and Samson stayed with me, as if knowing tomorrow was the day. The next day, he mustered up some strength and heaved his bloated body into the car, signaling, "I'm ready. It's time." I stayed in the vet's waiting room as my mom, once again, stayed with the dog. Two strangers consoled me; they knew exactly what was going on without me saying a word.

I adopted Angel after fostering her for three months through a local cat rescue, and she was all mine, until Derek came into the picture six years later and won her heart as well. Angel was with me through a cross-country move to New York and back, and the death of my mother.

Angel was my traveling companion, at ease in cars, subways, trains and planes. At parties she could be found among the throng of people, soliciting pets or simply soaking it all in. She never, ever hid. Her death, though not unexpected (she outlived her prognosis by a year), gutted me. She was the first pet that was solely my responsibility. Thus, she was the first pet I had to make the decision to euthanize.

For months, I marked the weekly anniversary of her death, refused to watch anything but comedies, and swore up and down that when a song came on the radio with the word "angel" in the lyric, she was saying hello. (Note: I still believe this.) I refused to order Chinese food for delivery on Sunday evenings because we ordered Chinese food for delivery on a Sunday evening—and Angel died the next day. I cried when I heard Alison Krauss perform "Angel Flying Too Close to the Ground" at a concert a month after Angel died. I experienced poignant, if somewhat perplexing, feelings of longing and sadness when I'd see parents with infants or young children, for it drove home the point that I no longer had a "child" to care for. I put on a brave face, but I was a wreck until the day—eight months later—we adopted two new cats from a local rescue. Ladybug and Mama Kitty are the soothing balm my heart desperately needed, and their presence, I believe, was divinely orchestrated.

I've experienced the loss of human loved ones, including both of my parents, but somehow nothing quite jolts me like the death of a pet. Maybe it's because we cannot talk to them about death. Maybe it's because of the painful awareness their lives are so much shorter than is fair. Maybe it's because oftentimes we are the ones who need to make the decision to end their lives.

"It's so unfair!" my friend Cindy, who put down her beloved dog just nine months before I put down Angel, said to me soon after Angel died. It is, so unfair.

Each time a pet dies, I fear I won't be able to love the next one as deeply as I did the one that just passed.

And yet, each time I do.

Each time I do.

After receiving her master's in journalism from the University of Kansas, Elena (Ellie) M. Macaluso returned to her native California and worked as a staff writer and editor for *Sacramento* magazine just shy of 15 years. She left the magazine to spend two years in New York City where she explored her roots (Macaluso's parents were both born and raised in New York City) and ticked off Bucket List items galore, including running the New York City Marathon.

Macaluso returned to California in 2015, got a proper state job, and continues to work as a freelance writer. In addition to *Sacramento* magazine, her work can be found in *Inside Publications*, *Mysterious Ways* and on Clark.com, the website of Atlanta-based consumer advocate Clark Howard.

Her work includes profiles, poetry, essays, short stories, full-length features and blogs. Macaluso resides in Sacramento with her boyfriend, Derek, and their cats, Ladybug and Mama Kitty.

BORN IN A BOAT

M.L. HAMILTON

I'm on my way to becoming a crazy cat lady. I know this, my family knows this, and anyone who comes to the house knows it. I currently have three cats. Of course, that's a relative number because who knows what might come walking down the street tomorrow.

My oldest cat, Salem, was an acquisition on the way to a family dinner. We stopped at the pet store and left with a six-month-old black cat because he melted into me when I picked him up. I have never regretted that impulsive decision because there has never been a cat like Salem. He's raised six puppies and kittens to be respectful, loyal citizens of our house. My sons used to carry him around their necks like a mink stole. Guests have threatened to steal him from me, and during a tarot reading, the reader remarked that having Salem sit on the cards was like having an ancient soul overseeing the proceedings.

My second cat, Figaro, came to me when I dropped my youngest son off at elementary school. Figaro was an abandoned kitten and the vet told me that if I hadn't picked him up when I did, he'd probably not have lasted the night. Figaro has always believed he should be an only child. He finds it endlessly distressing that he has to share our house with other creatures he deems unworthy. Sometimes I worry that Fig isn't completely right in the head. For years, he stole loaves of bread off our counter, and one time I caught him walking away with an entire pound of frozen chicken in his mouth, looking like a jaguar taking his kill up into the jungle trees.

Our third addition, Panda, came into my life in a very

traumatic fashion. One night I got a call from my neighbor that a cat had had a litter of kittens in his boat. He couldn't get the kittens out because he was allergic to cats. By the time he told me about them, the kittens were almost three months old and wild. My sons and I tried and tried to get them to no avail. When one of the kittens was hit and killed in the road, I knew I had to take action.

I got a humane cat trap and set it up on the side of my house where they often came to eat. The first night we caught Maddie, named for Madison Bumgarner, a pitcher with the San Francisco Giants. Maddie was a sweet, black and white kitten who immediately let us handle her.

The next night we caught Panda. Panda was a terror. She spat, she hissed, she slapped at the cage. When my son was trying to transfer her into a bigger kennel, she escaped and climbed into the engine of my car. When I tried to get her out, she bit me. We had to trap Panda a second time, which just added to her terror.

One of my students adopted Maddie and last I'd heard, Maddie was living her best life. However, I knew no one would take Panda because she was so feisty and I feared the pound would put her down, so I resigned myself to keeping her.

However, keeping a cat who screamed, hissed and slapped was not going to be easy. Winter was coming and she couldn't stay in the garage in a kennel. We moved her into the downstairs bathroom. As my son was bringing her in, Panda slapped and screamed at him. In frustration, he yelled at her to knock it off. I watched the whole thing, wondering why the hell I was bringing a wild animal into our house.

I set up a pet carrier in the shower and gave her food and water. She huddled in the back of the carrier and refused to come out. I'd go in a number of times a day and sit on the floor, just talking to her. The whole time I was in there, she'd growl at me.

Salem tried to come in the bathroom with me. He'd hover at the door and the minute I opened it, he'd dart inside, but I was so afraid she'd hurt him, I'd make him leave. If I'd only understood that he knew better than I did how to best handle Panda.

A week or two went by and the only progress I'd made was that she didn't growl at me when I came in to talk to her, but she still wouldn't come out of the carrier. If she was out when I opened the door, I could see a flash of white dart into the carrier again. By this time, Salem had gotten more and more insistent that he should be let inside.

I finally agreed and he immediately dashed into the carrier with her. I was in a panic because I was terrified she was going to attack him in a confined space and really do some damage, but I knew if I reached in there, I could cause even more harm.

When nothing happened, I chanced a look inside the carrier. Salem had stretched out and Panda was curled against his side, purring. I'd never heard her purr before. Over the next few days, whenever I went in to talk to Panda, Salem came with me. At first, he'd crawl into the carrier with her, then he stayed outside, letting me pet him. Gradually Panda came out, and over the course of many days, she began letting me pet her as well.

It's been five years since Panda came to live with me. She is now my sweet princess, who regularly falls into a deep sleep on my lap. I feel so honored whenever she lets me hold her because I know the level of trust it's taken for her to get to this place. She may have been born in a boat, but if you were to see her now, you'd think she was the Queen of the Nile with her faithful companion, Salem, by her side.

ML Hamilton teaches high school English and journalism in Central California. Since her earliest memory, books have been an integral part of her life, so pursuing a career teaching what she loved came naturally. However, she always dreamed of publishing her own novel.

That dream came true. Her first novel, *Emerald*, was published by Wild Wolf Publishing in 2010. Since that time, ten more books in the World of Samar series have been published. In 2013, the Peyton Brooks' Mysteries were born, allowing her to branch into a new genre. After seven novels in that series, she moved the main character into the FBI. In 2014, she began the Avery Nolan Adventures, an urban fantasy series set in beautiful Lake Tahoe.

In addition to teaching and writing, she has three sons, two dogs, and two cats. And a stray rabbit that sometimes resides under her deck.

MAXI

SCOTT CHARLES

Maximus Canis. Maxi.

Maxi's fur was warm. His nose was wet, and he had floppy ears.

If Ray listened carefully, he could still hear his mother and father reminding him to be good to Maxi. "Maxi is your true friend, so don't mistreat him," they would say. "Make time for him, don't ignore him and never ever, ever hit him. Because he loves you," they told him.

You could tell by the picture that Maxi was a good dog.

The stuffed dog that sat on Ray's desk didn't look like Maxi, but that was okay, because Ray didn't mind. When Ray had asked, "What kind of dog is Maxi?" his father had said, "Well, we're not sure."

But Ray discovered Maxi looked like the old RCA Victor dog, and the Buster Brown shoes dog. He told his mom and dad, and the three of them laughed together.

Those were good days.

Ray had his room set up so it was easy to see all the things he loved when he was lying in bed. If he turned a bit, or shifted his glance one way or the other, or tilted his head a little, he could see everything – except out the window. He had to get up to do that.

Over there was the *Starry Night* poster, which was one of his favorite paintings. And over there, in the corner, was a small collection of stuffed animals. He had a dog, a panda, a giraffe, a lion, a monkey, and a unicorn. Sometimes he would sleep with the stuffed dog, holding it tight until it got warm, snuggling up to it and pretending it was alive.

On the bureau sat the picture of him and Maxi, and that

was his absolute favorite possession.

Sometimes he would take the photo out of the frame and look at the inscription on the back. "Ray, 3 ½ y.o." it said in his mother's handwriting. He would close his eyes and run his fingers over the picture, then the inscription, and try to imagine his mother and Maxi. Sometimes he could feel their warmth.

In the photo it looked like Maxi was huge, but that was because it was taken from behind the two of them when Ray was a little boy.

They were sitting side-by-side, and he had his arm around the dog's shoulder, like two close friends sitting together in a garden – his mother's garden. He wore shorts, the kind that had straps that go over the shoulders. His legs were crossed. His sandals were visible. He wasn't wearing socks

Ray closed his eyes and reminded himself he had taken care of Maxi, and that was a good feeling.

On the shelves over the desk there were smaller stuffed animals, figurines, a snow globe, and a few books. Also, a wooden Tic-tac-toe game, a Rubik's cube, a pair of fuzzy dice, plus a few hand puppets. And a birdhouse built of sticks, something he had made at summer camp. The birdhouse was stuffed with straw, and pieces stuck out from the little entrance. Right next to the birdhouse was an old alarm clock.

If he felt like it, he could get up and look out the window and see the tops of the trees and look out over what used to be the garden. He didn't want to, not just yet. He had to go slowly, or he would lose his focus and the story would end. He didn't want it to end, so he kept still.

He could hear the echoes of his mother's voice.

His mother would say, "Come on Ray let's go outside. You can help me garden." Sometimes his father would join them.

The clock ticked and the hand moved, but not quite far enough. He could feel time shifting.

Maxi had short hair, white mixed with black. Ray's father had said maybe Maxi had a bit of Dalmatian in him. His father explained how animals inherit traits, and people did too. It was in their blood. That's where the secret to life was, in the blood.

Maxi would come up and put his nose in Ray's neck, or nudge his hand. Softly, just to let Ray know he loved him. His mother had told him that's what it meant when Maxi behaved that way.

He remembered most of it. And even if he didn't remember it exactly, it was still true. It made him feel good to think about it.

His mother had stopped gardening. When was that? After Ray was a bit older. Her back bothered her. It must have been when he was in first grade, just out of kindergarten.

Maxi had a big tail. "Like a scimitar," his father had said. His father had taught him how to be good to Maxi. Don't tease him, don't make fun of him, and don't mock him.

It was important for Ray to make time for Maxi. It was okay to play with the other kids, but he had to come home and play with Maxi, too. 'When you love someone, even if it's a dog, you make time. Maxi loves you, and he trusts you," his father had said. "Don't betray that trust."

There was something about the way his father had said those things, not in a harsh way, but very serious. The way he had put his hands on Ray's shoulders, then hugged him – Ray thought the intensity was odd, somehow out of place, as if his father had been desperate.

Ray had begun to sense something was changing, or was going to change, but he didn't know what it was, or even how he knew anything was actually going to be different. But he knew things were not the same as they had been. He just didn't know why.

When Ray had gotten a bit older, it was his job to take care of Maxi. He would fix the dog's breakfast, and then play with him in the yard or at the park. He would occasionally give him a bath, or clean his paws when it rained so he wouldn't track mud into the house. Then in the late afternoon he would fix Maxi's dinner. Every meal was the same – kibble and canned salmon. Maxi didn't seem to mind that the meals didn't have much variety.

Ray knew he had felt the same way about Maxi as he did about his kid friends. Maybe even better, because he had taken care of the dog in ways he hadn't taken care of the kid friends.

After he had mastered the art of fixing Maxi's meals it was his job to make the coffee in the mornings. He was way too young to drink coffee, and he had to stretch to his tallest height to work at the kitchen counter, but his mother and father seemed to enjoy watching him manage the ritual of the coffee making.

First, grind the beans, and then fill the coffee pot with water. The next step was to turn on the flame and set the timer for seven minutes. Then, when the timer went off, pour the coffee into the coffee cups.

Ray thought making the coffee would make them happy, but it didn't. His mother always looked tired and his father was mostly silent. Ray knew it hadn't always been that way, and he began to wonder if it was his fault.

The picture of him and Maxi sat on the bureau. He could feel the warmth of the dog's shoulder.

Sometimes it seemed the day that picture had been taken had been the last good day Ray could remember. He wanted to go back to that day and see if he could start from there and figure out what had happened.

Instead he remembered a different day, the day his father had knelt down beside him, put his hand on his shoulder, and told him for the last time to take care of Maxi. His father seemed ill at ease, and he smelled different.

Ray didn't like to remember that smell. Or how his mother was always tired. After that was when they stopped talking to each other. Then there was no more gardening.

He could feel time shifting away from him. He gently

pulled it back.

He closed his eyes and rolled over.

"I love you Maxi," he said.

And Maxi's ghost put his nose, gently, into Ray's neck. "I love you, too," said the dog.

"So do I," said the ghost of his father. And the three of them took a nap.

A gentle breeze whispered through the open window and the lace curtains billowed into the room. It sounded like wings fluttering.

Scott Charles was born in the Midwest and relocated to California in the 1980s. He lives a happy life with his wife and his dog. He has just released a novel, *"The Illustrated Hen,"* which is available on Amazon.com. He is also the author of several plays, including *"Dinners with Augie."* You can see some of his other works on his website at www.libernetics.com.

THE SINGING STARS

ELLEN OSBORN

A father put his little daughter on his shoulders to take her on an adventure. He wanted to show her the night sky, to share the beauty of creation with her. He felt she was ready to discover the stars that light the nights.

The little girl loved to ride on her father's shoulders. He was so tall, the tallest person she knew, but when she was on his shoulders, she was taller still. The world looked so different from up there. She wrapped her baby hands in his thick dark hair, holding tight, trusting, and ready to go where he wanted to take her.

They only went as far as the back garden, just outside the kitchen door. When her father closed the door behind them, they stepped into another world. Not the familiar garden where she played every day, but a dark, quiet, sleeping world beneath a star-lit sky. If the earth was peacefully drowsing, the sky was wide-awake, filled with sparkling, brightly colored, shiny stars. So many of them they crowded the sky. It was as if the stars themselves were waiting to greet her.

Everywhere she looked there were more and more stars. Never had she seen such twinkling, friendly little sparkles. They looked so alive! Forgetting to hold on, she reached her chubby little arms as high as they would go. Surely, she could catch one – a red one? A blue one? Or could she catch one of the many points of white light that beckoned her? With their twinkling they appeared to move closer, then away, inviting her to join their dance.

And then she heard them singing, a rising chorus of many, many unearthly voices. Her father may have been trying to point out the patterns in the sky people call constellations, but the little girl only had ears for the song of the stars. It was as though they had waited an eternity for someone who could hear them sing their special song.

How her father got his little daughter to go back into the house and go to bed (it was past her bedtime) no one remembers. Her dreams that night were of her newly discovered world, one large enough to include all the singing, shimmering stars.

The little girl grew up. Now she could go outside at night to be with her stars whenever she liked and listen to their soothing song. It was her favorite sound. She knew now that other people did not hear the singing of the stars. She alone heard them sing, the rising and falling of their countless voices synchronized with their pulsing, twinkling light. Other people heard the sound, but knew it was crickets, signaling to their mates. She knew it too, but was reluctant to give up the magic.

One night this grown-up, but not all the way grown-up, girl decided she didn't like being different. Alone, she went outside into the garden. Staring up at the starry sky, she repeated to herself "it's the crickets, not the stars," until she had forever separated for herself the cricket's song from the light of the stars.

The stars now seemed more remote, fewer, and colder, as if saddened by her decision. They were now forever out of her reach. Too late, she realized her mistake. She had had a special, secret magic in her life until she had driven it away, just so she could be like everyone else. She would forever miss her private joy and connection with a world beyond our reach.

* * *

As an adult, she still enjoyed summer evenings under the stars with her new friends, those little crickets. Their magic is how they make such soothing music with their tiny bodies and how together they make a chorus, their songs rising and falling in pleasing unison. She found the beauty of nature could be better than magic.

Primarily a writer of nonfiction history, Ellen is the author of the recently released history of El Dorado County *A Lovely And Comfortable Heritage Lost.* She has also written historical articles for such periodicals as *Sierra Heritage, Around Here* and the *Overland Journal.*

Ellen has contributions in NCPA's two previous anthologies, *Our Dance With Words* and *Birds of a Feather.* A member of the Placerville Shakespeare Club, she helped research and write the well-received original presentation "*El Dorado's True Gold Notable Women's* Stories" in 2013.

A fourth generation Californian, she graduated from San Francisco State. After spending her work life in the Bay Area, she and her husband are now retired and live in Pollock Pines, CA.

Ellen is a member of the El Dorado Writer's Guild and Northern California Publishers and Authors.

LIVE LIKE A KID

DENISE LEE BRANCO

There's a new kid in town. He's an explorer and a natural-born entertainer. Give him and his pals a rugged mountain to climb and they're the happiest showmen around!

Those kids are the four-legged members of the 65th annual California State Fair's inaugural *Goat Mountain* exhibit. I was among the authors staffing the California Authors Booth this year when I got wind of this intriguing new attraction.

As a young, horse-fanatic country girl, I had been fascinated by a ranch in the foothills near my hometown where goats and horses occupied a field, in harmony.

While horses grazed, goats stood or lay atop old tree stumps and hilly pasture ground. Sometimes, we'd pass by at just the right time when the kids (the name for a baby goat under six months of age) were being kids, frolicking about.

I imagined the show those kids at the fair would give their audience—jumping, head butting, high kicking, uphill sprinting, and I just had to see it! I looked forward to being up close for the first time, to watch the kids.

My first chance to drop by Goat Mountain was on my second day at the Fair. It was about 1pm, and by then, the poor little kids were laying on the shaded ground at the foot of their mountain under the large canvas tent which covered the area. Square box fans were operating at high speed to help comfort the little ones. Mama goats (also known as a does or nannies) were on duty as playground supervisors, maintaining order.

I spoke with the young goat-herder and she said the kids

are usually much more energetic in the morning and late evening. (Understandable. I am, too.)

The Fair opened at 10 am on weekends. My shift on the last day began at noon. Perfect! I had a two-hour window to get to Goat Mountain and a chance to catch the kids in action.

My first stop was the authors booth where I unloaded and set up my space as fast as I could. I knew time was of the essence, since it was predicted to be the hottest day of the year so far, and break a record for Sacramento.

As I approached the fenced-in area, I noticed the show had already begun. The kids were having a blast, and they put on a performance that did not disappoint! I took photos (15 to be exact) and chuckled at their antics the whole time. Every "baa" brought a smile to my face.

I stood in awe at the display before me. Clearly those kids were having the time of their lives, hopping around, sprinting to the mountaintop, play-fighting, and posing for their admirers. I swear one cute little guy stood still on purpose when he saw a camera in my hand.

My writing genre is inspirational nonfiction. Inspiring people has become my purpose. There's nothing more satisfying to me. I was trying to think what I could offer that would be inspirational about baby goats.

You know what? It's simple. We all need to live like a kid! Set aside time to play. Do something that brings you joy every single day. Don't let fear stop you from climbing mountains. Most of all, seize the moment like somebody left the barn door open!

Denise Lee Branco is an award-winning author and inspirational speaker, who continues to believe, dream, and overcome so those who meet her recognize the possibilities within them. Denise's first book, *Horse at the Corner Post: Our Divine Journey*, won a silver medal in the Living Now Book Awards.

A member of several literary and publishing organizations, Denise has served on the Board of California Writers Club-Sacramento and is a past Vice-President of Northern California Publishers and Authors (NCPA). She has been a contributing author in two Inspire Christian Writers' anthologies and three NCPA anthologies.

Denise is currently working on her next book(s). She lives in Northern California, and besides writing faith-filled inspirational stories, she loves spending time with and spoiling her three rescues.

Follow Denise on Twitter @DeniseLeeBranco and visit www.DeniseInspiresYou.com to learn more.

THE ALASKAN ADVENTURE

ELAINE FABER

George had saved all year to join Charlie and Danny's annual elk hunt into the Alaskan wilderness. With luck, at least one of them would be successful. After saving a couple of steaks for the family freezer, he'd donate the rest of his share to the town's homeless shelter.

"Buckle your seatbelts. We're coming in for a landing," the pilot said as the seaplane descended. Feeling lightheaded, George breathed into a paper bag.

The tiny blue patch surrounded by green became a small lake in the midst of the forest, 200 miles from the nearest Alaskan town. The seaplane hit the water and skidded to a stop. Charlie pushed open the cabin door. A gust of pine-scented mountain air whooshed in. "Look out, Alaskan elk, here we come!"

Danny pulled the plastic air valve on the inflatable raft. The bundle toppled through the cabin door, *swooshed* as it dropped six feet onto the lake and expanded into a viable craft sufficient to tote the hunters and their gear ashore. Within minutes, the three men unloaded supplies, hunting gear, and an emergency two-way radio, their only means of communication with the outside world until the plane's scheduled returned. "See you in four days," the pilot called.

Once on shore, the men spent the next hour haggling over the printed directions for assembling the tent. Finally, the structure was pitched and a campfire built. Patches of melting snow nearby suggested that spring came much later in the wilderness, than in Seattle.

George spent a fitful night, his imagination magnifying the sound of animals skittering through the underbrush. Just past dawn, the fearless hunters broke camp, pulled the labels off their new camouflage pants and shirts, and departed for the big hunt.

George stumbled through the underbrush about fifty yards to Danny's left, rifle at the ready, trigger finger a-tingle. Adrenaline pumped courage into the mighty hunter, whose only previous encounters with wild animals had been with a relentless gopher in the backyard and an angry gray squirrel gathering nuts in the park. Having no desire to become separated from his mentor, he kept a close watch on Danny's red-checkered shirt.

Wuwwaaahhh! Wuwwaahhh! Danny blew on a bugle elk call, intended to convince an unsuspecting bull elk that his soul mate was right around the next corner. Not exactly sporting, and who knew if it was even legal in this neck of the woods?

George stumbled on. Just before noon, the sun glinted off something in the bushes. He hurried toward it. Lord! "Hey guys! Over here. Come see what I found." He pulled tangled bushes off a plane, half-buried in the underbrush. Its scorched metal revealed it had burned upon impact.

Animal scratches on the door suggested wild animals had tried in vain to breach the cabin. George pried open the door. Skeletal remains lay sprawled across the steering wheel. A bony hand still gripped the stick. Empty eye sockets seemed to stare through the cracked windshield. Fire had partially scorched the interior. From the skeleton's condition and the tangled underbrush nearly covering the plane, the crash looked to be several years old.

Danny ducked his head inside the cabin and shuddered "Must have gone down in a storm." He reached across the skeleton's lap and hefted a faded leather satchel from the passenger seat. "What do you suppose this is?"

"Lemme see it." Charlie leaned his gun against the wing and took the satchel. He snapped open the catch. "Hey, check this out! It's full of cash." Discovery of the leather bag squelched the desire to continue hunting for a love-sick elk.

The excited men dashed back to camp to reconnoiter their next move. They sat around the campsite that night, one question leading to another.

Where had the money come from? The fire had obliterated the ID markings on the satchel.

Who was the pilot? Apparently, his personal effects had burned in the fire.

Were they obliged to return the money? Who would they give it to? *Uhh...*

George expressed sorrow for the pilot's family. Someone must be grieving the loss of their loved one.

Charlie chided George. "Don't be a namby-pamby. For all you know, the money was stolen and the insurance company has already covered the loss. Finders-keepers–losers-weepers." He counted the cash and piled it into three equal stacks of $72,465.

Fingering his share, temptation quickly overcame George's sympathy for the pilot's demise. He could pay off his credit cards, take a vacation, and start saving for their kid's college.

Danny fanned some of the bills. "We'll go back to the plane in the morning and pull the brambles back over the wreck. Somebody might still be looking for it." He turned away, unable to meet George's disapproving gaze. Dark clouds covered the mountain, and thunder rumbled in the distance.

The storm made landfall later that evening. The men hunched over a campfire that sputtered and steamed. Lightning flashed, thunder rolled, and buckets of rain sluiced down, dripped through the tent and soaked their sleeping bags. Around 3:00 AM, the men had had enough of Mother Nature.

"We passed a cave about a quarter mile from the plane," Danny muttered. "Let's take what we can carry to the cave. We'll come back in the morning and get the rest." He stuffed his share of the damp money inside his shirt.

Charlie crammed the radio inside the empty leather

satchel. "Maybe it'll stay dry in there."

As the storm raged, the three miserable conspirators carried their guns, bedrolls, and the satchel with the radio into the mouth of the cave. George found a few dry sticks and made a fire. They stripped down to their underwear and spread their clothing and the damp bills along the sides of the cave, hoping by morning, things would be dry. Even the thought of the money didn't improve their dampened spirits. The discouraged men stretched out beside the fire and tried to catch a few winks.

Bats and vermin scuttled in and out, making sleep difficult. George drew his cramped body into the fetal position and wrapped his arms around his legs. His dreams were filled with leering skeletons rising from the airplane, a bony hand stuffing wads of money down his throat, strangling him. Would the night never end? At last, the cave lightened as the sun crept up.

Whuff! Ruff!

George's eyes snapped open. *What was that?* He sat up. A dark lump at the rear of the cave, previously assumed to be a rock, moved. A head appeared, its mouth open, sharp, jagged teeth snapping with rage. *Great God.* George shrieked, "It's a mother bear with a cub! Run!"

Danny and Charlie jumped to their feet. Stumbling over each other, the three raced from the cave into the chilly dawn. They stopped thirty yards away, shivering and shaking, to assess the situation.

"Our money is still in there!" Charlie grumbled.

"Not to mention our clothes." Danny rubbed his arms.

"Don't forget the radio and our guns!" George hopped up and down.

A roar from the back of the cave reaffirmed their concerns

Charlie wrung his hands. "Danny. This is your fault. Go back and get our stuff. It was your stupid idea to sleep in the cave."

Danny shook his head. "Oh, no! It was your brilliant

idea to strip off our clothes and spread them around the cave."

George stared at the ground. "It was all our faults. We're being punished for stealing the money from the plane."

"We got no food, no clothes, no money and no way to call for help. Someone's got to go back in there. We'll all freeze to death if we stay out here." Leave it to Charlie to state the obvious.

"Just what do you suggest, knucklehead?" Danny scowled at his partner in crime, beating his hands on his arms, trying to return the circulation.

Danny gathered three dry weeds, snapped the top off one and leveled the three between chilled fingers. "We'll draw straws. Short straw goes in and gets the bear's attention. The other two follow, grab the guns and shoot the bear. At least two of us have a chance to survive. George. You pick first."

George reached out a trembling hand. He ran his finger over the three straws and then pulled back his hand. Choosing wrong meant he'd have to face the bear. He thought of his wife and child. They might be planning his funeral this weekend instead of visiting his dad at the rest home. He reached out again and touched first one straw and then another.

"Draw one, already," Charlie snarled. "We haven't got all day. I've got goosebumps the size of New Jersey."

George held up a finger, his concern for the baby bear overcoming common sense. "Wait! I'll go. I've got a plan. You guys follow me in. Don't shoot the bear unless she attacks. I'll keep her busy while you grab our stuff." George pulled off his skivvies and undershirt, wrapped and tied them around the end of a stick. Naked as a jaybird, and with chill bumps prickling his body like a giant pickle, he tiptoed into the cave. Danny and Charlie, bent double, crept a few paces behind. A roar came from the rear of the cave. George rushed to the fire, still smoldering in the cave, and inserted the bundle, hoping the glowing embers would ignite the makeshift torch before the bear attacked. And, that his torch would burn long enough for the guys to grab the gear.

The clothing-wrapped stick burst into flames. George danced and waved the blazing underwear over his head. He flung his arms around and rushed toward the bear. Startled by the blazing stick and a gyrating, naked man, the mother bear rose onto her hind feet and snarled. George hurled the blazing stick at the bear and screamed, "For the love of God, grab the gear and run!" The bear dropped to the ground as the burning stick touched her paw. She howled and lumbered forward. George turned, grabbed his jacket and raced into the sunshine, the bear close behind.

"This way, George!" Danny yelled from halfway up a nearby tree. Charlie's face appeared through the leaves further up. Even with a head start, it was apparent, that with a crazed mother bear after them, the men needed both hands to climb, for as sure as God made little green apples, the rifles, and the radio in the leather satchel lay abandoned on the ground.

George raced for the tree. Clutching the jacket between his teeth, he grabbed Danny's hand. Danny hefted him onto a lower branch, just as the mother bear bore down on him. She reached her front paws up the tree and then sat on the leather bag. Saliva dripped from her mouth. Murder flashed in her eyes. George slipped on his jacket and rearranged his bare bottom on the sharp branch. "Don't suppose you thought to grab my pants?"

Danny nodded toward the clothing scattered on the ground. "Sure did. Right down there. Help yourself."

"That didn't work so well, did it?" Charlie muttered.

"*Uh*, guys?" George pulled off a handful of leaves and fitfully tossed them at the bear. "Didn't I read somewhere that bears can climb trees?"

"Oh, Lord," Danny mumbled. "You better hope this bear can't read."

"So, now what, George? Any more, bright ideas? It was your bright idea to spare the bear. I wanted to shoot her."

"I guess we sit here and wait for her to leave. At least you've got a jacket." Charlie grumbled from the upper branch. "A lot of good it did to grab our guns and then leave them on the ground." He wrapped his arms around his chest and shivered.

"Stop complaining At least you're wearing skivvies…" George grimaced and shifted his bare bum on the branch.

"Trade you my tee shirt and $10,000 for your jacket," Danny muttered.

"Fat chance!" George pulled his coat down in the back and slid it an inch beneath his tush.

George looked up at the sound of a plane rumbling in the distance. Did they dare hope? Their plane wasn't due for three days. Why would it return so soon? Sure enough, the plane dropped below the tree line and landed on the nearby lake. Hoping they could be heard a half-mile away, George, Danny, and Charlie yelled until they were hoarse. Throughout their noisy performance, the bear ambled a few yards away, stopped and lay down, preventing the scantily dressed and shivering hunters from climbing down.

At the sound of men crashing through the underbrush, the bear scurried back into the cave, brought out her cub and lumbered away. As soon as she was out of sight, our heroes hurriedly climbed down the tree, and were pulling on their britches when the crew came into sight.

Their pilot waved toward the half-dressed hunters. "Hey, you guys, what's going on here? A party? *Heh Heh!* I thought you came to hunt elk?"

Trying to explain amidst the guffaws, George leaned down to zip up his pants. "There was this bear in the cave, see…and it chased us out, and we had to climb a tree."

"A bear, you say. Sure, there was. *Heh! Heh!*" The crew leader grinned. "That's why you're all half-dressed? Your pilot reported seeing a possible downed airplane when he dropped you off. Guess what we found? A missing drug lord's plane!" His gaze settled on the leather satchel. "And, from the looks of this bag, you fellows found it, too." He snapped open the lid, reached inside and pulled out the radio. "That's odd. Thought sure it would be full of money."

Charlie, Danny and George swapped anxious glances, and then all three started talking at once.

Charlie raised his hand to silence his co-conspirators. "Here's what happened. Money got all wet from the storm. We spread it around the cave to dry out last night. It's still in there."

The team leader nodded. "I see. Mighty nice of you, going to so much trouble to dry it out. Any other fellows might have been tempted to forget to report the crash. I guess you planned to turn it over to the authorities as soon as you got home. And, I'm sure you'll want to donate the reward to a worthy cause, right?"

"You got that right." Charlie zippered his pants and tucked in his shirt. "There's a reward, you say? Now, that's nice. We figured there might be a reward. We were discussing which worthy cause to donate it to when we met up with this bear, weren't we, guys?"

The team members exchanged glances, grinned, and wiggled their eyebrows as they gazed at the half-dressed hunters. "A bear, you say. *Uh-huh.* There's something *bare* around here, that's for sure." He chuckled. "Don't worry. Whatever happens in the woods, stays in the woods, right, fellas?"

Elaine Faber lives in Elk Grove, CA with her husband and four feline companions. She has published three cozy Black Cat mystery novels; stories partially narrated by Black Cat. With the aid of his ancestors' memories, he helps his *person* solve mysteries and crimes. The fourth cat mystery, *Black Cat and the Secret in Dewey's Diary* will be published in September, 2019.

Black Cat's Legacy
Black Cat and the Lethal Lawyer
Black Cat and the Accidental Angel

Three humorous WWII fiction novels followed. Fighting the war from the home front, elderly, eccentric Agnes Agatha Odboddy exposes homeland conspiracies and NAZI spies during WWII. In this humorous series, the reader finds historical facts and delights in Mrs. Odboddy's pranks.

Mrs. Odboddy Hometown Patriot
Mrs. Odboddy Undercover Courier
Mrs. Odboddy And Then There Was a Tiger
Email: Elaine.Faber@mindcandymysteries.com

Website: www.mindcandymysteries.com

ENOUGH OF THE PIG PUNS!

CHRISTINE L. VILLA

It was summertime! The zoo was once again crowded with kids of all ages. All the animals were singing and bopping inside their cages, except for me.

"What's the matter, Peggy Pig?" asked Elvis Elephant.

"Are you sad because you are not *hogging* all the attention?"

"Maybe she's upset because she finds herself des*pig*able. Nobody is taking a *pig*ture of her!" teased Tyler Tiger.

"Or maybe she is *boar*ed out of her mind!" Henry Hippo said, laughing his head off.

"Enough with the pig puns! I'm not *swining* or taking things for *grunt*ed..." I said in a sarcastic tone before continuing, "I actually appreciate that the children are here to visit us."

For once, I wanted to hear someone say something nice about pigs. This morning I heard a lady yelling at her husband, "Don't eat all of the popcorn! You're such a *pig*!"

"It's so hot today! I'm *sweating like a pig*!" an old man, wiping himself with a handkerchief, complained from a distance.

Then, just an hour ago, I heard a teenager scolding his little brother, "You're so *pigheaded*! I told you not to roam too far or you'd get lost!"

Why were there so many mean expressions about pigs? *Fat as a pig, pig face, pig out, pig it, make a pig of oneself, squeal like pig.* And so on...

"I wish I weren't a pig," I mumbled.

I trudged towards the pond and looked at my reflection. What if I were to put a bright pink bow on my head? Maybe it would make me feel better. Then I remembered the expression—*putting lipstick on a pig*. Oh, boy. Even if I did put a pink bow on my head, I would still look and feel ugly.

What if I just closed my eyes and dreamt that the long list of pig expressions was vanishing into thin air? Yeah, sure, and *pigs can fly*. There goes another expression!

There had to be something out there that would make me feel good. I was determined not to *wallow* in self-pity. I needed to think positive. First, I had to ignore all the silly pig remarks. Then, I looked around with a smile on my face. It was difficult pretending I was happy, but I faked it until I believed I really had something to be happy about. Before I knew it, I was beaming at every guest who visited the *pig sty*. *Never in a pig's eye* did I think it could be possible!

Just before the day ended, I spotted a little girl over the fence. As she was skipping all the way close to the pig sty, her *pigtails* bopped up and down.

"Mom, please hold my *piggy bank*. I want Dad to give me a *piggyback* ride!" she said. Her peal of laughter made my heart sing.

So, there were pig fans out there after all! *If that don't beat a pig a-pecking!* I looked up at the little girl and was soon in *hog heaven*.

Christine "Chrissi" L. Villa founded *Purple Cotton Candy Arts*, a small business that started out exploring her creativity in the field of arts and crafts and later expanded into publishing her children's picture books. She has published nine children's book titles since 2014, two of which won first place in the Northern California Publishers and Authors (NCPA) Book Award Competitions in 2018 and 2019.

Recently, *Purple Cotton Candy Arts* started offering publishing services to other aspiring children's authors and publishers.

As a gifted poet, Villa's haiku and tanka have appeared in numerous online and print journals worldwide, she's garnered several awards, and has published her first poetry book, *The Bluebird's Cry*.

Chrissi is founding editor of *Frameless Sky*, the first haiku and tanka journal, available on DVD, and *Velvet Dusk Publishing*.

She is also the new editor of Ribbons, the official publication of Tanka Society of America.

THE YARD

ERIN G. BURRELL

The Red-tailed Hawk eyed its prey.

Nestled against the warmth of the aggregate patio, a Mourning Dove rested and absorbed the sun's rays into sandy-buff plumage. The only sound, a gurgling waterfall. The noise bubbled as water slipped and fell over stone-steps into a pond below. The orange and white splattered Koi swam peacefully.

The hawk's head tilted; one black orb zeroed in on its target. Eyes closed, the dove continued to laze in the morning light. The hunter hunched down and lifted from the limb into flight. The eyes of the dove blinked open. It sprang off the patio, wings beating the air. A rapid-fire *coo, coo, coo* could be heard as it made a slender escape.

The large hungry raptor didn't appear to be upset that its meal had vanished. It glided in an unhurried manner to a Pistachio tree in the distance to start the ritual all over again.

*   *   *

The yard used to teem with life. Many birds darted in and out of the vegetation. Some that flitted about were: Scrub Jays, American Robins, Northern Mockingbirds, Plain Titmouse, White-crowned Sparrows, Juncos, and Black-chinned Hummingbirds. Their joyous songs started much too early, and caused me to slam windows. After sufficient beauty sleep, I enjoyed watching my feathered neighbors taking recess in my waterfall. Sparrows frolicked and splashed water onto their backs. When done bathing, they shook violently, sending sprays of moisture skyward. Light caught the myriad water droplets, morphing them into tiny glittering diamonds carelessly cast about.

Western Gray squirrels also called the backyard home. They scampered across fence rails, using them as highways, racing to their next order of business. Small paws grabbed tree limbs to exit the roadway, where they could be seen dashing from branch-to-branch. Most times the squirrels kept to the trees. With bodies flattened, they hugged the trunk of the Pistachio tree, playing tag. One chasing another in dizzying fashion, round-and-round, claws digging into bark. At varying intervals, the squirrels stopped in unison, winded, gulping for air. Then, as if hearing a starter's gun, they bolted, raced upward through the tree, across branches and pounced onto the roof. The pounding of multiple clawed-feet could be heard until the next player was tagged.

The din and activity of the yard filled me with delight. From my sofa, I stared outdoors taking in the colors of the jungle-like retreat. The view was as mesmerizing as the flames of a fire. The reds and oranges were replaced by greens and browns. Palm plants and ferns planted too close together swayed in Delta breezes and bowed to three tall Redwoods. The pond sprawled beneath the evergreen canopy.

A lone Pistachio stood majestically in the center of an elevated oval-area, bound by a two-foot high river-rock wall. The tree's outstretched arms provided a welcoming shade to all below. Ivy and other low-growing ground-cover surrounded its base. Slate stones created a small patio in the front portion of the oval. Two cushioned chairs were placed so they overlooked the pond.

This was my sacred space.

A place where I could close my eyes, and listen to the sounds of the plants as soft winds caressed their foliage. A place to hear the tattling of squirrels, or the gentle trilling of birds. This sanctuary brought me a peace like no other. While meditating in my chair, my breath and heartrate slowed, calm spread throughout my veins, and time no longer held meaning.

*   *   *

The first time I noticed the Red-tailed Hawk, it was perched in the Pistachio tree. I thought the event magical and believed the sighting was a blessing. A nearby squirrel wasn't of the same opinion. It chattered a loud rant, sounding an alarm. Several birds squawked and took up the squirrel's siren. The hawk didn't seem upset by the commotion, only bored. It took to the air with an easy grace.

One day when I went to sit in my favorite spot, I discovered discarded feathers floating atop the ivy. A friend had become a meal for the hawk. Gazing up, I glimpsed plumage stuck to a branch, the apparent crime scene where the Scrub Jay had been plucked clean. It felt like someone dear had been murdered. I was heartsick and powerless.

Not long after, I witnessed feathers floating down from the sky like snowflakes, making no sound as they drifted onto the cement walkway. I ran into the yard as the hawk leapt from the sturdy bough, wings spread wide, and talons wrapped possessively around its victim.

Last week, I caught an image out of the corner of my eye. I turned and looked out the slider to see a squirrel lounging on the aggregate. We were separated by fifteen feet. The animal met my gaze. The squirrel's position mimicked that of a Playboy Centerfold. Upper body supported by arms that extended to the ground, paws spread like hands. The lower body rested seductively on one hip, the fur-covered belly faced me, legs spread. I'd never witnessed a rodent, or any critter for that matter, posturing so.

I opened the slider and stepped onto the walkway. The squirrel turned its upper body away from me, and with only the use of its front arms, attempted to get away. The lower half of its body remained strangely on its side, feet and tail dragging lifelessly. My heart dissolved. I wanted to lay hands on this fragile creature and heal it. I believed it had been dropped from a great height, or its back had been broken in a mighty grip or struggle.

The Western Gray exerted a vast amount of energy to move. Every few feet, it stopped to rest, mouth open and panting. Its chest rose and fell in rapid beats. When able, it would drag its dead weight a bit further, then rest again. The small animal made it to the pond, and vanished beneath a shrub.

The vision of the helpless and twisted squirrel haunts me.

There is no longer cause to slam windows shut, as only two types of birds remain in the yard. The hummingbirds still zip around the feeder and take cover in the Pistachio tree. They may be too fast and small for the Red-tailed Hawk. That predator made my backyard a restaurant, and it gorged itself on the inhabitants. It consumed many a meal high in the branches of the Pistachio tree. It was easy to know where the hunter had dined because feathers littered the ground below. Another song quieted.

Death is like the Red-tailed Hawk. It steals in on soundless wings, and plucks loved ones from your home. The longing for those absent creates fissures in the heart and fills a dwelling with a deafening eerie silence. Another voice quieted.

Erin G. Burrell lives in Elk Grove, California. Her memoir, *That's Why You're Here, A Journey from Grief to Metaphysical Awareness*, was published in 2018. She is an Intuitive Empath who loves to connect to spirit through Tarot Cards.

Working only from a place of love and light, Erin has a gift for giving and receiving messages on a soul level. Her readings have helped many individuals seeking answers about their personal path.

She is a natural teacher and brings a wealth of life experiences to her readings. Her educational background and 25-year career with the state have given her the opportunity to mentor and work with people from all walks of life.

You can contact her through her website at egbtarot.com or through email at eblucky58@gmail.com.

THE ETHER SQUIRREL INCIDENT

JULIE BEYERS

Every family has those stories that...you know the ones...get repeated year after year at family reunions and other gatherings. My family has them, too. One of my favorites comes up each year because it was during a college spring break, the week before Easter, when one of our family's most memorable stories took place.

My sister, brother and I were all home on break at the same time – a rarity in our usually diverse schedules. I was enjoying kicking back and playing tennis with friends who were also home for spring break. My brother was doing whatever it was he was doing. My sister had 'homework' from one of her college classes. It was that homework that sparked '*The Ether Squirrel Incident.*'

My very bright, science major sister was taking a course titled *Natural History of Vertebrates*. Her instructor figured that his students would learn more about small mammals if they knew enough of the animal's behavior and habitat to be able to catch them. The assignment...make ten "museum quality study skins" of small vertebrates to present to the class before the end of the semester.

My sister came home from college with enough supplies for two or three of the necessary skins and an initial goal of obtaining a California vole. Why a vole? I have no idea, except they were less common than the average field mouse. I volunteered to help in her quest for small critters.

Our home was on the south side of town in a late 1950s era subdivision; street after street of homes built by a single contractor. The house was on a cul-de-sac tucked in the back of the subdivision. Behind the rows of homes was an open field, a couple hundred feet wide, extending about a mile on either side of an access street to our part of town. Beyond the field was a frontage road that paralleled the freeway.

The open field seemed perfect for the placement of traps. My sis and I walked there and started scouting the area for any sign of small rodents that could be caught in the mouse traps we were carrying. We had seen rabbits in that field a number of years back when our dad demonstrated how to use the bow and arrows which had lived in our garage for years. It had been an awesome demonstration, and fortunately missed the hapless jack rabbit he aimed at. None of us kids really wanted the bunny to die.

We didn't see any rabbits, but discovered animal trails among the spring flowers and grasses. We found several promising spots to set the small traps. As my sister was setting a trap, three neighborhood kids rode by on bikes. They looked to be junior high age and, not surprisingly, all were boys. We had survived being outnumbered by the boys on our street, and memories of their rowdiness flashed through my sister's thoughts. She picked up the trap she had just set, then explained she doubted the boys would leave our traps alone. The trapping plan for this location was abandoned.

Fortunately, a family member had a connection with the manager of the local Water Treatment Plant. My sister was granted permission to access the plant property to set traps, so we drove to the treatment plant at the edge of town. A couple of traps were set early that day amongst the grasses and weeds in an undeveloped part of the property. The plan was to return in a day or two and check the traps for bodies.

The trip driving back to the Water Treatment Plant was full of anticipation. Would there be success in the traps? Would something be trapped but still alive? I had lots of questions but was scared to ask them. However, seeing my sister in her full academic scientist mode, I was amazed by her confidence, and thrilled to be part of this effort.

I don't remember who thought it was a good idea, but

the family dog, Nemo, accompanied us to check the traps. Nemo, a Keeshond mix, looked a bit like a small, really furry wolf except his tail partially curled up over his back. His attitude was always that of a great protector – he would place himself between us kids and any unknown person, strain at the leash and bark if unsure of the individual. His bark was deep and low like that of a German Sheppard or a Rottweiler. He never bit anyone, and once introduced, could come darn close to licking you until you dripped with dog spit.

Dog in tow, we checked the traps. Both the first and second traps were sprung, bait missing, and empty. The third trap, however, successfully captured a small brown critter. Not the vole we were hoping for, but a field mouse that apparently wasn't quite as smart as the others.

Initially my sister was thrilled. But examining the mouse, we learned that it was missing the last third of its tail. The stated goal of the homework was to collect and prepare 'museum quality' examples of animals. A short-tailed mouse didn't fit the profile for the class.

My sister sighed and I remember her saying words to the effect of "This mouse died because of me, so I will use it just as if it were perfect." The mouse went into a glass jar in the back of the car. As was common practice for researchers collecting animal specimens, the jar already held a small ether soaked rag. The ether was there to kill any fleas, lice or other vermin that still remained in the fur or on the skin of the now-deceased mouse.

One small mouse was a help towards my sister's class requirement, but where else could we go? We had talked about finding another place to set traps before we left the house that morning. It was probably during that conversation when our mom suggested that - being 'just girls' - we should bring a baseball bat with us 'for protection'. We left the bat in the car at the Water Treatment Plant because we had Nemo with us.

The creek that ran along the frontage road near our house was the other spot identified as a potential habitat for critters we could catch. Every living thing needs water, so we reasoned there ought to be critters living by the creek. With the mouse already in the family station wagon, we loaded up the traps, Nemo, and ourselves. Heading out from the plant, we passed a city police car heading into the plant via the only access road. We noticed the vehicle but didn't give it much thought.

Parking along the frontage road, we decided to survey the creek area before hauling any traps out. One of us took Nemo, the other had the baseball bat. We had discussed possible animals that we might encounter and decided the bat might be useful to knock out a sewer rat or other animal we might find...in case we startled one as we were checking the area. We found what might have been an animal trail headed toward the creek below us. At the creek's edge we looked up and down the gurgling brook for any sign of small critters.

Deep into our task and with the noise both we and the dog were making, we didn't hear a car pull up and park near ours. Apparently a car door opened and closed but we didn't hear that either. Perhaps it was the freeway noise or traffic on the frontage road, not our talking that prevented us from knowing about that other car. However, the voice calling from the top of the creek bed sliced through the morning air like a shot. "Hey, ladies. Could you come on up here, please?" A glance toward where the voice came from startled us. You don't say no to the cops, not in our town, not in any town.

We ascended the trail, curious why a cop was there. We looked at each other but didn't say a word. Once top side, the all-business lady officer advised us they had received complaints about two people possibly breaking into cars with a baseball bat. Obviously concerned, with her hand on her gun - a standard police practice - she asked for an explanation and for us to identify ourselves.

My sister handed me Nemo's leash and I held on while he barked and strained at the end of it. I now had both the baseball bat and the dog, as my sister took a few steps forward before introducing us and explaining our mission.

I think the cop actually laughed. She visibly relaxed, took her hand off her weapon, then introduced herself. I don't recall her name, but do remember the conversation she and my sister had.

The lady officer had been a biology major in college and had worked in that field before changing careers to become a police officer. They bantered back and forth about science stuff that sounded interesting but made no sense to me, an accounting major. I did manage to put the bat into the car sometime before the back-up officer drove by. Instead of arresting us for being a public nuisance, the understanding officer chatted with my sis, viewed the mouse in the jar, our traps and other supplies in our car, and petted Nemo. She also shared that the patrol car we saw at the Water Treatment Plant had been dispatched there because staff at the plant had called about trespassers. My sister explained about the arrangement she had with the plant manager, who apparently forgot to tell his staff.

Several more minutes of science-based and college-related conversation took place before the officer was radioed to take another call. As she was leaving, she suggested we find a less public place to trap during the rest of spring break. I don't remember the discussion my sister and I had on the way home, except we were relieved our run-in with the police went so well.

At home, that mouse in the jar went into a brown paper bag and that bag went into the refrigerator. This was necessary to keep the mouse from spoiling and ruining the pelt. The brown paper bag was to keep our mom from having a heart attack when she got home from work to find a mouse in her refrigerator, staring back at her.

The next morning, I went off with a friend to play tennis at a court across town. I needed to be back by 11:00 a.m. to go with my siblings to meet our dad at his office, then go to lunch. I don't remember much about our tennis game, but I knew it was fun to spend time with my friend, whose college was more than six hours from mine.

My friend did the driving and on the way home I could hardly believe our good fortune at another's demise. There, in the far-right lane, lay a road-kill squirrel, fat and fresh with no tire marks on its little body. I practically screamed, "Pull over! Pull over! It's a squirrel! It's a squirrel!"

She had no idea what I was yelling about but pulled the car over without squishing our prize. I quickly explained as we exited her car, then we pondered how to get the squirrel home. We didn't want to touch a flea-infested squirrel, not even a beautiful gray squirrel. A rather nice hand towel from the backseat became a squirrel wrap and the bundle went into the trunk. Jackpot!

Arriving home, my sister was fetched to deal with our surprise. She was thrilled, but concerned…we needed to be leaving for lunch. There wasn't a glass jar big enough for the squirrel, so it was stuffed in a metal coffee can with a plastic lid, an ether soaked rag was added, and the squirrel joined the mouse in the refrigerator. A quick 20 minutes later we three kids were in the station wagon and off to meet dad. I'm pretty sure my brother did the driving; they sure weren't going to let their kid sister drive.

We didn't think about the squirrel beyond our sister telling Dad about it and her plan to process her two specimens the next day. However, when we arrived home from our leisurely lunch, all bets were off. Opening the front door we were slammed with the pungent odor of ether permeating the house. Mortified, my sister retrieved the squirrel from the refrigerator, but it still needed to be kept cold. The only other cold space available was the garage refrigerator/freezer. With hopes that a freezing temperature would hinder the ether smell, we put the squirrel-laden coffee can in the freezer. The brown paper bag and mouse went into the refrigerator in the garage.

Mom was not amused when she got home from work. She was even less amused when the meat planned for dinner that evening reeked of ether. I think we went out for pizza that night. The next morning, the milk for our cereal and in our glasses tasted like ether. My brother and I refused the vile, white liquid. My sister toughed out a few swallows before she gave up trying to drink the stuff.

From just after breakfast until well after dark, we didn't see our sister. We only heard her cuss a few times while she processed the mouse and then the squirrel behind her closed bedroom door. How she survived the smell, even with her bedroom window open, was a testament to her dedication and personal resolve. Mom delivered meals to her room. While sis labored over the critters, Mom threw out anything in the refrigerator that wasn't in a sealed glass jar. Lettuce, carrots, grapes, cheese, hot dogs, bologna – everything was 'sniff tested' for ether and it all ended up in the trash. It was after my sister went back to college that Mom realized the ether had permeated everything in both the house and garage refrigerator and freezer compartments. It was weeks before Mom shared that information with my sister.

The end result of all her efforts was outstanding. Mounted on a board more than two-feet long, the squirrel was perfectly placed to show the sheen of its coat and grip of its sharp claws. The squirrel looked like it was running, its beautiful tail streaming out behind it. The mouse, on its own board, was demure and petite, its stubby tail curled slightly behind it. Both were amazingly lifelike and so carefully created.

The trick now was to get them back to college, making sure they survived the multi-day drive. The three students traveling back to college were committed to getting my sister's animals back to campus in great shape, so all her work could be recognized.

The beautiful gray squirrel became a celebrity on the drive back to college. Perched on top of several suitcases, the mounted squirrel was clearly visible through the window on the left side of the Volkswagen Squareback car my sister's classmate was driving. The mouse proudly held a similar spot on the right side of the car. Other drivers honked and waved; some even took pictures. The stares, honks and waves continued through three states as they returned to campus.

So, each spring, as Easter approaches, the *Ether Squirrel Incident* is remembered and the tale is told to anyone who hasn't heard it. My sister has gotten over her embarrassment about the whole thing, but she has yet to be the first to share the story. She takes the annual ribbing in her usual good-natured way. Today, she is an amazing scientist and an even more amazing sister. Thanks for the memory and the story, sis.

In her work life, Julie Beyers did accounting, wrote contracts and grant applications, and other administrative stuff. Her editing skills were utilized by all of her employers. She led an evening writers' group, *The Placer Word Miners*, in Auburn, CA, for five years, and authored an article in the May 2016 issue of The Nugget Magazine, for the Sacramento District Dental Society, as part of her work to improve the oral health of young children.

A Sacramento area resident, Julie dabbles in poetry, short stories, and does editing and grant writing for others. She has a memoir piece in *Birds of a Feather*.

Julie is available to authors for consulting on any length project and to non-profits to develop grant application content and strategies. Contact Julie through her website, www.juliebeyers.com.

INTRODUCTION TO CHICKENESE

SHARON S DARROW

B ackyard chickens are popular all over the country. They're good for the environment, great for your yard and garden, and cheaper than a stress reduction therapist --- well, maybe. If you don't do your homework before establishing your flock, better have that therapist on speed dial.

When Holly, my favorite niece, suggested we get chickens, I was sure my husband's resounding "NO" would reverberate throughout the county. To my shock, Stan thought it was a great idea and started researching chicken coop kits. He was thrilled to find a lot of cute designs that cost less than $300. I'm a vegan, but thought having our very own birds to lay eggs would pay for the coop in no time, and be healthier, too.

First lesson in Chickenese – always read the fine print. The chicken coops we fell in love with had the dimensions spelled out in a tiny font at the bottom of the page and would have been great for an oversized Barbie house. Any poor chickens stuck in those things would have no room to move, and maintaining and cleaning them would have me doubled up like Quasimodo. After much more searching, Stan found a suitable coop design on Google with an initial cost of less than $300. Of course, that amount was for the downloadable design plans and hardware only. By the time he purchased all the materials, we calculated it would take about 8,000 eggs from the girls to cover the cost of their coop. And that didn't count the cost of the Epsom salts and pain patches for his sore muscles after the construction.

Chickens are supposed to be low maintenance, right? Holly told us how easy they are to keep, and the suburban chicken bible, *City Chicks*, made getting started sound easy. A sturdy coop, some shavings on the bottom to absorb the droppings, bag of food, fresh water, and we'd be good to go. Ha! The Chickenese translation proved to be a bit more complicated.

First, we wanted shavings so the coop would be ready for the birds. Easy-peasy, right? Nope. Can't use cedar because it's toxic for chickens. Pine is fine, but aspen is supposed to be better. The very best, according to the chicken experts online, is hemp. But to afford hemp shavings I'd have to be earning at least seven figures. Sorry birds, but we settled on pine since it was one-fifth the cost of aspen and one-tenth the cost of hemp. Stan will have to consume lots and lots of eggs if our girls are ever going to earn their keep.

Before bringing the chickens home, I went to the neighborhood feed store and asked for a bag of chicken feed. The young man asked if I wanted pellets, crumbles, or scratch. Scratch? I just wanted food for the darn birds. Then he asked me about their ages and sex so he could recommend the feed type with the best ingredients. I'm not this picky choosing foods for my husband.

Once we decided which kind of food to use, well, actually, after we gave up trying to compare the merits of the various types and called Holly to find out what she used, we had to buy the right kind of chicken feeder. Then the best water containers ... and can't forget the oyster shells ... and how about a bag of freeze-dried worms for a treat? He even recommended a couple of wooden eggs to show the chickens where to do their thing. That's when we drew the line.

We were so excited when the big day came and our beautiful chicken coop welcomed six feisty, big hens. Holly chose birds that were already friends, so they could settle in and form a new little flock. Two long weeks of keeping them contained so they could bond together and with their new home, then we turned them loose in the yard and our Chickenese education began.

Our dog, Ellen, is a Great Dane – but she's also a digger. Just before the new girls were let free, Ellen dug a hole in the middle of the grassy lawn. Didn't take long, those huge feet created a two-foot crater in the dirt in minutes. We'd yelled at her and made her stop, but hadn't yet filled it back in before the birds found the hole on their very first day loose. We'd been told chickens like to take dirt baths and even watched Holly's birds roll around in a hole they'd dug in their coop. So cute, but not truth in advertising.

Our hens found Ellen's hole and jumped in to remodel. How good could three skinny toes on each foot be at digging? Ha! The dirt looked like a rooster tail behind a ski boat. The hole got bigger, wider, and deeper. At one point three birds were barely visible above the edge. They looked adorable digging and wiggling around. Poor Ellen. She got yelled at for digging, but the burrowing chickens starred in Facebook videos. As soon as we decided to leave the hole for a permanent dirt bird bath, they never used it again.

Holly and the book, *City Chicks*, told us the birds would molt each year. No big deal, they'd just look scruffy while they lost some feathers and grew in new ones. True, but not the whole truth. Molting can last months and the yard looks like you sacrificed some feather beds; plumage all over the lawn, stuck in your plant and tree branches, low drifts lining your house walls. Stan mowed over them, thinking the blades would take care of the problem. Instead, the feathers were ripped and ragged, with the pieces spread even farther, and when he used the blower to clean off the patio, swirls of feathers drifted over the grass.

And let's talk about our lawn after the chickens moved in. One of the selling points for suburban chickens is that they provide natural fertilizer for your lawn. Eliminating chemicals is great for the grass. But the definition of "natural fertilizer" is chicken poop. Couldn't be more natural, and the chickens will spread it everywhere – your grass, your patio, any rocks or decorative walkways. Your lawn will be healthy, but you will never again walk barefoot in the grass. Or on the patio in the dark. You'll have to hose off your patio much more often too, and I guarantee one of the birds will sneak back and make a fresh deposit before the concrete is dry.

We fell in love with our birds and bragged about them like any proud pet parent. They were so cute, so fun to watch, so friendly. We were sure that sharing them with friends and family would be another great experience. I invited Ann, my best friend of twenty-five years, her daughter, Candi, and Candi's two children, Xavier and Anna, to come visit the chickens. They were excited and eager to pet and feed our sweet birds. After all, other adults had come over and seen the chickens and admired them; this would be even more special

Remember Chickenese? Another rule is, never take anything for granted. When Ann and Candi followed me into the yard, the birds just watched them. As soon as the two kids came into sight – and these are two very well-mannered children who've been raised to respect animals – the chickens started squawking at the top of their lungs. They ran and flew all the way to their coop as fast as legs and wings could take them, and kept screeching and flying around inside as long as the children were in sight. You'd swear those kids were carrying axes and a cast-iron skillet. So much for sweet, friendly birds. The kids' feelings were hurt, and it was downright embarrassing.

When I told Holly, she assured me they had never acted like that before. Great, now it was our fault for turning normal birds into neurotics. *City Chicks* doesn't have a chapter on that.

The antisocial girls calmed right down once the children left. Rotten birds, making two great kids feel bad. After that, no more kid company for the girls to torment.

Stan and I've settled into our "household-with-chickens" routines pretty well. First thing each morning, one of us has to go open the chicken coop door and let the birds out.

They're always lined up in front waiting, cackling their complaints that we'd wasted hours of sunlight sleeping. At the end of the day, one of us has to close and secure the coop after the girls have settled themselves on their roost. If we dare leave the house for a social event in the evening, one of us has to carry a lantern out to lock up when we come home. God forbid we forget, because then I have to get up out of a warm bed, put on my bright red chicken boots, and traipse out to the coop to lock them in. All kinds of creatures love chicken dinners – raccoons, skunks, rats, possums, non-vegetarian humans – so the birds have to be protected from predators.

After a couple of months, we were confident chicken parents. And then one day, Lady Cluck wouldn't come out of the nesting box. All the girls spent time in the nesting boxes to lay their eggs, but then they rejoined the others out in the yard. But Lady Cluck stayed put all day. No egg, but she wouldn't come out. By the next morning, I was in a panic. She'd stayed in the nest all night instead of roosting with the other hens, and was settled in for another nesting day.

My years of kitten rescue experience told me that an animal that wouldn't eat or drink or get on its feet was very sick. Heartsick, I checked her over. Eyes clear and bright, no nasal or eye discharge, breathing sounded normal. Next would be a check for dehydration – but how do you check skin covered by feathers? And Lady Cluck is a Cochin, which means she's covered with feathers from her beak to the tips of her toes. I even put my head next to her back to listen to her breathing – she was not thrilled with that – which sounded normal with no rasping or wheezing. But she would not get out of the nest.

What to do? First, I told my husband it looked like our favorite girl was very sick and might not make it, since it was Saturday and I couldn't get her to a vet until Monday. And then I'd have to find a vet that treated chickens. Her symptoms were serious, but somehow we'd have to keep her going until then. Our hearts were broken. We treated all the girls the same, but we both loved Lady Cluck best for her sweet temperament and cute body that looked like a feather-covered soccer ball.

No choice but to call Holly and share the terrible news. Perhaps she could give us some advice on what vet to use and how to sustain our poor baby until she could get medical help. I hated picking up the phone and leaving a message admitting I was a chicken failure.

When Holly called back, she laughed at me! The dire symptoms for kittens and cats just meant that Lady Cluck was "broody". Broody? Yes, she just wanted to hatch some chicks and was staying in the nest waiting for babies. Quite a feat without eggs or a rooster. It seems Cochins are quite broody and we could expect her to take up to three weeks to return to normal. And she might go broody (don't you love it, getting the Chickenese down?) a couple times a year. All we had to do was make her leave the nest at least once a day so she'd eat and drink a little.

Panic averted, pride injured, but at least we're learning. Who would have thought keeping chickens could be so complicated? How in the world did old-time farmers manage without specialty books, chicken vets, and experts available by phone? When I voiced these questions to my parents, my dad laughed and told me they never did anything with their chickens. The birds found their own food, sheltered where they wanted in the barn, and left their eggs all around for the kids to find. I asked him what they did when a chicken got sick. His answer was a chuckle, and a chopping motion.

Guess our girls are lucky to be modern chickens. Pets all the way, destined to live long, pampered lives and die of old age!

Sharon Darrow is an entrepreneur, business owner, award winning author, public speaker, and an expert in caring for neonatal orphan kittens.

Her books, *Bottlekatz, A Complete Care Guide for Orphan Kittens,* and *Faces of Rescue, Cats, Kittens and Great Danes,* are about animal rescue. Sharon's two memoirs, *Hindsight to Insight, A Traditional to Metaphysical Memoir,* and *Tom Flynn, Medium & Healer,* are inspirational, and her fifth non-fiction, *Navigating the Publishing Maze, Self-Publishing 101,* is a training manual about publishing.

Sharon also writes historical fiction, inspired by her maternal grandmother: *She Survives,* and *Strive and Protect* are the first two books in the Laura's Dash series.

Sharon firmly believes that life just gets better and richer, the longer you live. Her personal motto is "Find harmony within, then all things are possible."

TROPHY SHOT

RONALD JAVOR

Mostly, it was the searing heat and stifling humidity. Combine that with the swirling dust, pungent odors, hordes of buzzing, swarming insects, a cacophony of both large and small bird calls, monkey screams, and the sounds of unseen animals chumphing and scurrying away, all of his senses were overwhelmed.

Jimmy Clark stopped walking and stood still to get his bearings. He was a retired US Army sniper and tracker, over six feet tall with short dark hair, and despite being employed as a state park ranger, usually sitting in a truck or an office, he clearly was in great physical shape.

He felt warm sweat trickling down his back under his shirt and backpack, and every time he swatted a bug on his face, his hand came away wet with blood and sweat. None of this discomfort was unexpected: he was in central Africa after all, in Rwanda to be exact, on a safari he had planned and prepared for over many months, and had anticipated even longer. This was the fourth day of his hunt in the deep bush country, and only two days remained before he might have to return empty-handed to Idaho.

It was a little past noon, and he'd been slogging along barely detectable animal trails through the dense jungle, since just after sunrise. The high, thick canopy of trees blocked most of the light, but not the heat. He reached a location the safari guides had assured him was a gathering place of several extended families of great silverback mountain gorillas, and finding one of them was the reason he had organized this safari. In the last five years, he had sought, seen and shot all the other African "greats", but never a gorilla.

Jimmy left the jungle guides back at the campsite early that morning. They wouldn't be needed for tracking, because he knew what signs to look for and he knew several people walking together, even trained hunters, would create too many smells and sounds as they traveled through the forest. Those types of disturbances could spook the gorillas who would either hide or, if they felt threatened, attack before he was able to get set for his shot.

The African guides warned him about the dangers posed by his search, especially since this was an area with gorilla families, including youngsters, whose mothers would protect them. He also had to be on the lookout for other predators that were common there. But he assured the guides he was capable of handling any threat: hadn't they already seen him capture a large lion they had stumbled upon before it had a chance to charge or disappear?

Jimmy started walking more slowly and deliberately, following the scant trail that widened into one that was more traveled. Suddenly, he broke through a wall of thick underbrush and emerged in a small clearing. He stepped forward slowly and quietly, carefully studying the ground around him. He saw the signs he'd been looking for: partially eaten fruits, large paw prints, clumps of hair on the bushes, and piles of scat. He bent over to inspect the scat, and saw it was still soft and smelly so he knew he was not far behind them.

Without moving again, he straightened up and listened carefully. There were none of the characteristic roars or chattering of gorillas, but just in case one appeared suddenly in the clearing, he reached over his shoulder and readied his gear. He stretched the strap so it was comfortably tight, calibrated the range finder, and made sure it was loaded and ready to shoot. He realized he would have only one opportunity for a clear shot before the gorillas either scattered or threatened him, so he also set it for automatic continuous, or burst shots.

Despite the heat, Jimmy suddenly felt a chill run down

his spine. For the first time all day, there were no sounds surrounding him. The birds, the screaming monkeys, everything had disappeared, or become silent. He silently wondered, had his movements or spoor in the clearing scared them away? He slowly tiptoed backwards out of the clearing, intending to hide between two tall trees. Then, as he turned around to look for a place to kneel and set up, he saw his target.

A couple of yards away, stalking *him*, watching *him,* quietly crouched on *its* hands and feet, was an enormous silverback gorilla. He could see it was old and had battle scars on its face and ears. And like him, it stood still, staring. The gorilla looked both fierce and angry. Suddenly, it rose up on its hind legs, bared its large sharp teeth and let loose a roar that sounded like a jet engine.

Jimmy's senses jumped into high alert, and everything around him suddenly started to move in slow motion. He saw the enormous gorilla threatening him, but also noticed the gorilla had two babies just behind it that it was protecting.

Then the gorilla lurched forward towards where he was standing. Without thinking, Jimmy flung his gear and his backpack on the ground, turned around, and started scrambling away through the bush. He felt branches and bushes tearing at his clothing, knocking off his hat, and scratching his face and arms as he ran around trees and over downed logs. But those obstacles were nothing compared to the roars and the sounds of limbs crashing behind him as the gorilla chased him. Despite the pain and obstacles, Jimmy didn't slow down or look back until he no longer heard his pursuer. When the noises of the chase stopped, he figured the gorilla decided it would not leave its young unguarded any longer. He eased into a slower lope, not yet ready to just walk.

Out of breath, shaking more from exhaustion than fear, and unable to see clearly through his sweat-soaked eyes, Jimmy stopped to rest and regain his bearings so he could return to the campsite. He knew he had to walk towards the afternoon sun since it had been behind him when he set out that morning.

After several hours of pushing through heavy vines and trees, and just as the sun was beginning to set, he was dreaming about fresh water, food, and safety, when in the distance he saw smoke rising from the camp's cook fire. Finally, although relieved and embarrassed, as well as exhausted and thirsty, he stumbled and limped into the camp and found his guides and trackers waiting for him.

Even in the dusk, the guides saw his torn clothes and his cut and bleeding face and arms. They brought out the first aid kit, treated his cuts and bruises and asked what happened to him. He described how he'd found the clearing with its signs of recent use, how the gorilla surprised and threatened him, and how he managed to escape becoming a victim rather than a hunter. Sadly, he added that since he'd lost all of his equipment as well as his enthusiasm, the safari was going to have to end early and they would return to the nearby town the next day. He offered to pay them if they would go where he had been, find his gear, and return it to him in the United States.

Several months passed back home in Idaho before a large envelope arrived from the safari company. He paused before opening it, figuring it was just a letter informing him his equipment had not been found, but offering him another opportunity for a safari. When he finally opened it, the contents—a letter and several large photographs—slipped out. He looked at the photographs in amazement: they were close-up pictures of the two gorilla infants holding and staring at the camera he had dropped. They apparently had pressed on the shot button when they picked it up and it started automatically shooting pictures until it ran out of film. So, he *had* successfully shot a gorilla on his safari, even though it wasn't the one he'd intended.

The letter also said his camera equipment and other gear were being shipped together, so he could plan another photo safari to Africa.

Ronald Javor is an author of seven children's books about children who have barriers such as homelessness or disabilities and how they overcome them.

Three have been awarded NCPA honors. For over 40 years, he also authored legal briefs, legal contracts, and new laws, all related to housing issues. Having a safe "home" is a theme that runs through most of his writing.

When not working or volunteering for various local organizations advocating for or assisting homeless people, he lives happily with his canine and feline partners and enjoys traveling and outdoor activities.

For more on his children's books, see www.ronaldjavorbooks.com.

ONE GOOD DEED DESERVES ANOTHER

NORMA JEAN THORNTON

Was it fate, or sheer luck that he chose that exact moment in time to appear on the scene? Whichever, 19 October 2005 would be the luckiest day of that scrungy, skinny, sick little black kitten's life. Did he realize that as he blindly stumbled out from under the van at the same time Granny was moving the lawn sprinkler?

The kitten was sick. His face was a mass of streaked yellow and green globs of snot, some dried, some gooey. He sneezed uncontrollably, blowing even more flecks of slime all over the place, even on Granny. His eyes were almost completely glued shut and oozing with more yellow goopy stuff, but as Granny, with two fingers, gingerly picked up the tiny mewing bundle of gunk by the nape of his scrawny little neck, and held him at a distance, his motor started running and the loud purring began.

Granny and Papa had lost one of their three full-grown cats earlier in the year to diabetes, and had no intent to fill the void from his loss; two cats were plenty. When this little guy showed up, there was no desire to keep him. Besides – neither of them even liked black cats...at that time.

Papa had cancer and was worsening by the day – his trips back and forth to the hospital were becoming more frequent and the stays were getting longer. The last thing in the world either of them needed was a sick kitten to care for.

But Granny couldn't just set him down and go back in the house. Their two cats were already outside and headed towards him to take a sniff; for sure, they'd get sick, too.

Besides, if she put him on the sidewalk, he'd just come

back in the yard – if not that, what if a dog got him or a car hit him? Even if they wanted to keep him, which they didn't, there was no place to keep him separated from their other two cats.

To no avail, she wandered the neighborhood with the kitten, trying to find someone who would claim the pathetic looking little thing. Finally, she took him to their vet, hoping to find some gullible soul to take him. No takers, and the receptionist suggested the shelter.

There was no way she could – or would – do that; she couldn't willingly chance the shelter not being able to give the kitten away, and the possible consequences.

Granny wasn't a crier, but she went to the car with him and cried, out of sheer frustration. She had touched him. It was obvious deep down in the recesses of her being he was destined to be theirs, even as she tried to fight it.

She took the pathetic, constantly purring little bundle of scraggly black fur back inside, and instructed the vet to do whatever needed to be done to make him better. She'd be back to pick him up after Papa's chemo appointment, but before they closed. Granny would just have to find something to do with him – at least his face would be clean and he'd be easier to deal with.

Even though they had rescued their other cats, saving that kitten they eventually named Sirius Black (yes, Granny and Papa were Harry Potter fans), was possibly one of the greatest good deeds they had ever done, but there's another part to this good deed story.

That October incident also turned out to be the best thing that happened to Granny and Papa that entire year, but at the time, neither of them realized it.

Sirius Black was instantly, and totally, accepted by the other two cats from the moment they were exposed to him; possibly because he was kept in the brand new (so new that Granny had completely forgotten about it until she got back home with the kitten), totally empty, tall Tuff-Shed (with both radio and tv for stimulation, plus a fan, as well as blankets and toys, and plenty of food and water) the first dozen or so days he lived there.

Sirius became a curiosity to Dobby and Windy, his cat-siblings, as they watched Granny or her daughter and grand-daughter going in and out of that shed daily. Even though the cats had no contact with him then, they could smell him on the girls when they came out, after they had played with, fed, and medicated Sirius.

By the time he was brought in the house (after two full rounds of 7-day-each-antibiotics to clear up his severe upper-respiratory infection), Dobby and Windy were familiar with his smells and excited to finally get to give him a thorough "sniffing"…*all* over… Sirius, in turn, was so ecstatic about being out of that shed and having the company of the two cats on a continuous basis, he took to them as fish to water.

Each time Papa came home from his many overnight, or extended, trips to the hospital, Sirius stayed in the hospital bed with him constantly, mostly on Papa's chest, close enough for both to get benefits – a good ear scratching for the cat, and a wet beard-and-face-licking, in exchange, for Papa.

For the first ten days of what turned out to be Papa's final two weeks, Sirius did his own good deed by being a blessing to Papa while keeping him occupied and chuckling at the silly things all of the cats were doing because of the kitten.

Then Papa became too ill to even notice what was going on around him.

For the next three days, Sirius stayed right by Papa while the end neared, as though watching over him. Everyone commented on how the tiny new kitten had positioned himself as close as he could get, stretched full length at Papa's side, as if glued to him, while they lay together in the hospital bed in the den, until just thirteen days before Christmas.

That good deed continued even after Papa died, with Sirius a comforting distraction for Granny, and keeping Dobby and Windy busy playing.

For a full three weeks later, each night at bedtime, and

each morning at rising, Sirius slithered under the covers, alternately wrapping himself in Granny's arms, purring incessantly, and lovingly licking her mouth and nose area for a few minutes, before going to pester his two kitty-siblings.

Off and on during each day he was in and out of the house and back and forth in her arms as if to say "It's ok – I'm here for you in your time of need, just like you were there for me."

* * *

For years, Sirius continued to console Granny. He seemed to know whenever it had been an especially hard day for her, and would wrap himself in her arms each time, noisily purring, with a look of sheer satisfaction on his loving face.

It always worked.

Her baby sister called her Nonie, her great-granddaughter calls her GumGum.

Norma Jean Thornton, AKA Noniedoodles, a multiple County and State Fair award-winning baker, candy-maker and art-doodler, plus award-winning writing granny from Rio Linda, California, attempts to create her doodle-art, and dabbles with her writings at the computer, with unwanted help from her feisty cats.

lulu.com/spotlight/nonie lulu.com/spotlight/TheGrannysWritings
noniedoodles@yahoo.com

*"*Love Never Dies*" in Harlequin's Inspirational Anthology, A Kiss Under the Mistletoe

*Nonie's Big Bottom Girls' Rio Linda Cookbooks (4)

*Nonie's "Stuff" Cookbooks (Candy &...Stuff; Cookies...&...Stuff; Soups &...Stuff)

*Nosie Rosie's Diaries: (True cat diaries, written by The Granny & The Windy)
 (Years 1 & 2 of 15-years so far)

*Nonie's Cat Anthologies (Fun, not-so-fun, sometimes crazy short cat stories) 2 Volumes

*Nonie's Wet Kitty Kisses Anthologies (Mostly humorous Short Stories) 2 Volumes

*noniedoodles color books (artwork by Nonie's original doodles) Several Volumes

*Doodles the Dorky Dragon, in the Dorky Land of Noniedoodles

SENT BY AN ANGEL

DANITA MOON

The minute Chubba was born, we knew she was meant to be ours.

Born breech, she had the biggest mouth you've ever seen. Her mouth is the reason she received the name "Chubba-Bubba", Chubba for short. She and I locked eyes, and became buddies for life.

I raised her from a newborn Terrier-mix pup, and when she was a year old, the funniest thing was to come home daily, and find her nursing, right along-side the new litter of puppies. Her mother was looking at me with a 'Help me!' look.

Chubba was very protective of me, especially when it was bedtime. I would say "Bedtime for Bonzo," and she would shoot into the bed and do her nightly ritual of running down to the bottom of the bed, run back up, then plop her head on the pillow next to mine.

When we were in bed, anyone coming in that room had to turn the light on before entering, or they'd receive the meanest growl you've ever heard.

As the years passed, our bond grew. She loved to play with our other dogs, as well as the cats, but I'd always find her waiting for me at the door when I'd get home from school or work.

Leaving for college was the hardest thing I ever did, because I could see the sadness in her eyes, when she knew she was being left behind.

When I'd return home on the weekends, she would be happy, and we'd pick up where we left off, as though I'd never left, but when it was time to return to school, she would get that sadness in her eyes again. My mom told me Chubba would look for me for a couple of days after I left.

When I decided to transfer to a local college and returned home, it was like the life returned to her eyes and she acted like a puppy again, but it was short lived. I found her one day just lying in her bed, which was very unusual.

I took her to the vet and received the worst news possible. She had uterine cancer. I couldn't put her through all the treatments that wouldn't guarantee she'd live longer than a couple of months, so I made the hardest decision I ever had to make in my life. I held her as she took her last breath, and she knew she was loved.

We weren't looking for another pet. I, especially, wasn't, but a few months after we lost Chubba, we heard that a neighbor's dog had puppies. My mom went over to look at them, and I came home from school to a little golden retriever with the floppiest legs and saddest brown eyes, wearing a big red bow. She came running to me and just licked me to death. We named her Pokey, because she kind of poked along

I was standoffish at first, because I didn't want to get attached to another dog after losing my best friend of twelve years, but somehow Pokey wormed her way into my heart.

After a few months, something caught my eye on our security screen door. I had to blink to make sure I was seeing what I thought I was seeing. On the screen was the silhouette of Chubba. I felt as though she was telling me she could leave now that she had sent the right dog to take over where she left off.

To this day I believe Chubba was an Angel who sent Pokey to us so I wouldn't be sad anymore. Pokey was with us for many happy years, filled with a lot of fun. I still think of Chubba often, and have a new dog, Jet, who has the same markings as Chubba did, so I believe Chubba is somehow with me again.

Danita Moon resides in Antelope, CA. A Certified Proofreader, she also has a bachelor's degree in Business Administration – Accounting. She is an eclectic reader and reads a wide range of authors. She is also an advocate for Mental Illness Awareness and Suicide Prevention.

Danita spends her spare time with her family as well as her two dogs. She enjoys volunteering in the California Author Booth at the California State Fair every July where she gets to interact with fellow readers and authors.

ON THE PORCH WITH MISS LIZZY

BARBARA YOUNG

Quick, sharp taps on the window screen above my head. They seemed out of harmony with the cooing of the mourning doves and soothing sound of waves on the beach a mere ten yards away.

I shivered to alertness from my delicious night of sleep.

A scampering, slender, lime green lizard huntress, looking like a small dinosaur, pecked at the black mosquito morsels that were windblown against the screen., and snatched others from midair, with grace and precision.

In each direction, just outside the margin of her territory, were larger, even more prehistoric looking brown lizards. They spent more time doing push-ups and flicking their jagged finned-tails than catching mosquitoes.

As they lunged, she darted, chomped and gulped down her catch. The flirtations and challenges from the boys did not distract her. Breakfast was her focus, at least until her belly got full.

My exhale was forceful and irregular as a laugh shook my insides. My face tingled and warmed as my dimpled cheeks bunched up. This was a delightful way to wake up…in wonder, and without an alarm clock…just the sounds of breakfast in the making, backed by waves.

"You're a very lucky lizard, Miss Lizzy," I named her. "What a life you have being a beach lizard."

Inspired by Miss Lizzy's morning achievement, I got up and seized breakfast for myself—sun-ripened pink guava and salmon-orange colored papaya in a bowl of my home-cultured cashew yogurt and pistachio nuts.

Venturing from the cocoon of my open-air single-room

cottage, it seemed the soles of my feet suctioned slightly to the damp sea-sprayed, Caribbean blue-painted wood deck. I claimed a scenic position on the porch, swaying back and forth in the slick white painted ladder-back rocker. My skin tingled in the breeze as my loosely tied sarong playfully fluttered.

This is my favorite place on Earth...nestled under the centenarian tamarind tree and amidst the frangipani, yucca, papaya, hibiscus and orchids.

The sugar birds were going crazy dive-bombing the hanging half-shell of a coconut. There was no formal line for waiting one's turn. Just a frenzied cluster of happy yellow birds, squawking and flitting. The moment one emerged from the shell with its beak encrusted in white, several others swooped in to urge others out of the way.

Crackle...crackle, crackle...chip, scrape...bump...crackle... crackle, crunch. The sun was bright and the hermit crabs were having a scavenging rally in the cool shade under the deck.

Sounds of the gentle surf and the squeal of gulls called me to join them for some fun in the sun. I put on my new green bikini; a tropical plant pattern remarkably similar to the flora surrounding my cottage.

The pillow-soft beach sand was warm beneath my feet. Two lizards left very tiny prints as they scurried across the sand and onto a tree. I thought one looked like Miss Lizzy, but I lost them from view as their coloring quickly changed, camouflaging them.

At the waters' edge I stood on the dry sand, as we both awaited the next wave.

The view down the beach was of a scalloped lacey residue of foam on the wet sand. The waves gently rolled and seemed to tease the beach with multiple approaches before dashing onto the sand in varying reaches. A forceful gush of frothy water quickly covered my feet and continued to surround me. It rushed up my legs and body to spray me in the face. I was soaked.

A nearby gull laughed loudly as it flew by. I laughed with

it as the sand seeped up between my toes.

The water was clear and warm on my swim, and a school of blue tang accompanied me. There was a clutter of broken shells by the opening to an octopus den. Colorful sea fans gracefully waved with the undulating currents. Some had flamingo tongue snails clinging to them for a ride.

I felt buoyant and free like a bird defying gravity, suspended over the life beneath the sea.

After surf and sun, I lay in the hammock to dry off.

Soft, fitful scurrying movements in the tree caught my attention. It was Miss Lizzy. She was being chased by a boy lizard. Just as she established some personal distance, two other boys sauntered onto the scene.

It seemed the two newcomers were friends until Miss Lizzy caught their eye. At that moment they sprang into sparring position with one another. The original boy lizard was alerted, and began rapidly bobbing his head and doing push-ups.

This is like a three-ringed circus.

Miss Lizzy flicked her tail periodically as she looked upon the action as if at an arena where the chivalrous knights wrestled and flaunted their prowess.

"Ha Haaa!" I rooted out-loud for the boys, and cheered for Miss Lizzy to choose the one who would get her favor.

She casually wiggled and repositioned herself.

How could she not be excited?

Then one of the new boys walked away from the action. He climbed upon a broken twig that was illuminated by sunlight coming through the leaves of the tree. From under his neck, a beautiful vivid red fin appeared and retracted several times.

This was a bold and flirtatious act.

Miss Lizzy swooped her head in his direction and froze her posture.

She and I were both stunned.

He was the obvious winner.

After eavesdropping on the soap opera of Miss Lizzy's

life, I went in to my cottage to shower and get ready for the evening.

My appetite was minimal as I felt satiated by the day, so I only ate a light snack.

Later, I noticed Miss Lizzy was alone and busy on the seafoam green painted porch railing of the deck. I sat in the rocker and watched her dine beneath the hanging, once sugar-filled, coconut shell. Disregarding any manners, the cutest little pink tongue lapped up the bits of sugar scattered by the bananaquit birds earlier that day.

She really knows the ins and outs of this beach life.

Gazing at the foam aloft on the surface of the water following a breaking wave, I felt light, and eased into meditation.

A high-pitched hum…EEEeeeEEEEEee…I remained still.

eeeeEEEeeeEEEEEeeEEE…I gave a quick shudder of my head, left to right.

AUMMMMMMM…trying to stay in meditation.

eeeeEEEeeeEEEEEeeEEEEEEEEE…Swak! Got it, I hope the mosquitoes will not continue to bother me.

In my grogginess, I noticed the sun was lower in a now pastel painted sky. Miss Lizzy was on the balusters, plucking mosquitoes from flight. I mused at her skill, and that she seemed to stand by as I meditated. My lids slowly rested closed…aaAAAUUUUMMMMmmmm…

Abruptly, I roused from meditation with a shrill! Something with tiny, prickly things jumped on my leg. As I jerked my leg away, Miss Lizzy rolled onto the deck.

"Oh, Miss Lizzy, I am sorry. You surprised me and I did not know it was you."

She looked up at me.

How do I apologize to a lizard?

Just then I felt a small needle-like sensation and sting on my arm. I smashed the mosquito and just before I swiped it away, the answer came. I picked up the limp mosquito, between two fingertips.

As I reached toward her, Miss Lizzy postured slightly. I laid the offering of apology and friendship on the porch deck in front of her. Miss Lizzy cocked her head to one side and with her left eye, looked deeply into mine.

The black speck disappeared in a blink as Miss Lizzy swiftly snatched it up. She had received my gesture.

"Thank you for understanding Miss Lizzy."

She looked back and forth as if calculating something, then made a bold and daring leap of trust and friendship. She again landed on my leg.

This time I squelched my shudder, and marveled at both her bravery, and mine. I relaxed as I grew accustomed to the gentle cling and the tickle of her prickly feet. Miss Lizzy launched her opportunistic plans.

I observed the stars while Miss Lizzy stood watch.

There was a sparse swarm of mid-air dancing mosquitoes around my leg where Miss Lizzy perched. For the next ten minutes she repeatedly crouched and lunged…and dined on her private feast.

That night, as I relaxed into sleep, I recounted the many blessings from the day. I smiled, thankful for Miss Lizzy, my new friend and bodyguard, and looked forward to another extraordinary day on the porch, at the beach.

Barbara Young has a favorite place on a beach, similar to the one in *On the Porch with Miss Lizzy,* her 2nd publication in the NCPA's anthologies.

She is currently writing the second edition of her first nonfiction book, *The Heart that Rocks Health Care.*

She also writes poetry, children's stories and coffee table books that feature her photography.

Learn more at www.byoungbooks.com.

ONE

KIMBERLY A. EDWARDS

I said good-bye to my daughter, Elaine, on a Sunday in May as she got in the car to drive from California to Kentucky to study nursing. Her belongings filled every and crevice in the backseat and trunk. Already, in the early sun, I felt conflicted. My beloved middle child leaving: the child born between a willful sister and a coddled younger brother. She who listened to my rants, who never judged, who confided details about her dating life. With a mix of worry and excitement, I wondered if I should be traveling with her.

Gingerly strapped in the front passenger seat - Elaine's cherished companion, 17-year old chiweenie, Kaley. The little brown body shivered on a cushioned bed. She looked at me with a single brown eye. The whiskered muzzle, soft to the touch, bowed at the sound of my voice. She knew she was leaving home. I wondered if she knew what I knew: that I might never see her again. I suspected she had cancer. But of course, I did not tell Elaine. Today marked the beginning of a new era.

A month earlier, when I entered Elaine's room in my home, a bombshell awaited. A head cone tied to Kaley's neck revealed a covert procedure of which I had not been told. A specialized veterinarian had removed one of her cataracts. Elaine had not divulged this extravagant expense beforehand. I cried, "You did what?"

"I want her to be able to see in her final years," said Elaine.

"Who would pay thousands of dollars to fix an old dog's eyes?"

"Just one eye," said Elaine, her pupils receding into tears. "They couldn't save the other one."

"You're supposed to be economizing for nursing school."

"I want her to be able to see in her last years."

"The dog was getting around just fine. It's not as if the world went dark in one day."

"She's like my child. My only child."

The room fell silent, but for the grating of the head cone scraping the wire pen that confined Kaley. I knew that Elaine badly wanted to start a family. I, too, wanted that for her. But the aging dog tried my patience – barking, urinating, foraging through garbage cans in my condo. Kaley's sense of smell led her to where her eyes and ears no longer could.

On this Sunday of good-bye, I grappled with the emotion of a child leaving home in a car crammed to the windows. Would she be safe? Did she have a full view of the highway? Would Kaley distract her? Elaine had debated leaving the dog with me, but she decided to take her along to minimize "stress" – hers or the dog's, I wasn't sure.

They had been a pair since Valentine's Day more than a decade and a half earlier, when a mysterious basket addressed to Elaine appeared at my front door. No chocolate, nor flowers, but a soft brush coat topped by two frightened eyes and perked ears. I threatened to send the box back to the boy who purportedly delivered the gift. But when the pup emitted a low whine, as if calling to the child in the middle, I surrendered.

The brown-eyed dog became the brown-eyed girl's runway model. Kaley amused me in her many outfits: bridal gowns, pearls, sunglasses, biker hats, wig of orange braids. The dog with the duds chaperoned Elaine from wobbly teens to settled thirties.

Kaley became the thermometer for Elaine's relationships. If dates showed affection to the dog, the mercury shot up. A five-year liaison with a jerk who paid attention to Kaley bought him an extra 12 months in Elaine's life. In the end, Kaley outlasted him.

As the dog with the long body and short legs entered her golden era, I began to notice the special treatment lavished: brand name cuisine, color-coordinated layers of blankets, and recurring appointments, including with a dog dentist who pulled a tooth. Still, Kaley's deep bark echoed through my walls and over lawns. Fangs flared to bigger dogs who approached her treats. It was easy to ignore the sentiment that might drive an owner to pay a fortune to have cataracts removed.

Elaine teased me about being "heartless."

"How can you say this isn't the most beautiful face you've ever seen?" she would ask, pressing the canine's snout in my face to kiss, and pledge eternal love. I couldn't understand such devotion.

As time passed, my hair turned greyer. I added more highlights. Kaley's coat became more grey than brown. I had my cataracts removed. With the seasons rolling, whiteness spread over one of Kaley's eyes. I paid little heed to the annoying canine, much less to the clouded eye. I asserted "no" to buying a dog stroller or a ladder to help her mount the couch.

Soon Kaley's other eye turned white, inexplicably projecting a glint when light hit at just the right angle. At times I felt I stood in headlights. Hesitantly, I accompanied Elaine to the office of a dog eye doctor, who said he likely couldn't restore either eye fully, but that he could try, for a pricy fee. I tightened my purse strap over my shoulder as I felt the pleading from Elaine across the exam room. I wasn't about to throw thousands into a dog living on borrowed time.

While I never felt guilty, as Kaley's eyesight faded, her hearing dulled, and her bladder failed, I began to appreciate her fortune to have my daughter who bought her doggy diapers. I cut some slack for the 22-pounder needing care. I, too, might need that someday. I wondered how Elaine would manage Kaley's deteriorating health.

One winter night, when Elaine left for the evening, I heard Kaley toddle into my bedroom. No whine, no growl, no usual demanding yap. I expected her to spring onto my bed. I peered over the side of the mattress to find her reclined. Obviously she lacked the confidence to jump, or even to ask for help. In a gesture of weakness, I pulled the near-blinded dog into my arms. Relief passed through her body, even as her gaze stayed hidden behind the fog. When I awoke in the morning, a warm body curved around my hip where arthritis is setting in.

I realized that soon both would be gone from my home – the daughter whom I loved and the dog she cherished.

When the car departed that Sunday in May, I sensed that driver and passenger were entering an experience transcending the grind of wheels. Sharing the front seats, Elaine and Kaley represented two ends of time. One, starting; one, ending. My middle child knew what she wanted and was pursuing a goal. Kaley was taking the ride of her life, becoming one with her doting mother, my daughter, in a capsule of unity headed across the U.S.

Over the next four days, reports came from the road. Kaley starred in every text and photo. One restored eye was as good as two. The states passed like butterflies, California, Nevada, Utah, Colorado, Kansas, Missouri, Illinois, Indiana. After 2,225 miles, they reached Louisville, Kentucky. Within an hour, I received a photo of Kaley settled on her favorite blanket. The care given Kaley displayed the thoughtfulness of the middle child I was already missing.

When we say goodbye to a child, a part of us goes, too. We fret, we rethink, we review everything we ever did. But now I see that when a child pursues a direction, the unfolding adventure steels the mind and emotions for terrain yet to come. I don't know what will happen when Kaley passes to the other world. I, too, will be sad. But I am confident that Elaine will find the needed strength. I await her return, with Kaley, one eye, or both closed in stillness, daughter and dog, having seen a depth of devotion unknown to many.

Kimberly A. Edwards, president of the California Writers Club Sacramento, writes articles, memoir, and personal essays. She has championed writers for more than 30 years. In addition to having served as publisher of a monthly subscription newsletter for writers, she has written for *Writer's Digest* and other publications serving women, teens, specialty, and general audiences. Each summer she attends the Kenyon Review Writer's Workshop (literary nonfiction, hybrid). She is an alumnus of the Squaw Valley Community of Writers (fiction). She likes helping fellow writers turn memories into enduring stories. Currently she is at work on a book for the History Press. She has been a featured reader at Writers on Air. A member of the American Society of Journalists and Authors and the Independent Book Publishers Association, she likes to see writers pursue their dream and urges them to be persistent, keep fine-tuning craft, and never give up.

Kimberlyedwards00@comcast.net.

HOW TORTOISE FOUND OUT NAMES OF 3 PRINCESSES

3 PRINCESSES

CHILDHOOD TALE FROM NIGERIAN-IBIBIO FOLKLORE

EMMA UMANA CLASBERRY

The King Posed a Puzzle

Long ago in the forest, the king of the animals had three beautiful daughters. No one knew their names, except for the king and the queen. Even their cousins, aunts, uncles and close friends did not know their names.

Names of people were a well-kept secret. That was the way it was then, because parents were afraid it would be easy for strangers to steal a child if they knew the child's name. In that way, they protected all their children from being kidnapped.

When the three princesses grew up and were old enough to marry, the king wanted them to have as a husband the cleverest and the most intelligent animal in the kingdom.

So, one day, the king invited all the animals to his palace. He then said to them, "Whoever can find out the names of my three daughters can marry them, all three." In those days, it was okay for a male to marry sisters. "I will also give that animal many great gifts," the king promised.

The king gave everyone seven days to find out the names of his daughters.

All the animals grumbled as they left the palace. "This is the most unusual and difficult challenge," they said to one another.

But in their minds, they wanted to marry the princesses and get the great gifts from the king. Why? In those days, it was a great honor and prestige to marry the king's daughters. So, they did all they could to solve the puzzle.

"Oh! I have a friend in the king's family," some of the animals said. They went to their friends who were the princesses' uncles, aunts, nieces and nephews to ask for help. But those relatives could not tell them the princesses' names because they themselves did not know.

Those animals were very disappointed, but did not give up. They hoped to get lucky soon before the day came to tell the king his daughters' names.

For Tortoise, the king's puzzle was the rarest and most difficult he had ever faced in his life. He spent a number of days and sleepless nights thinking of ways to find out the princesses' names.

Like the other animals, Tortoise went to his friends who were the princesses' uncles, aunties, nephews, nieces and their friends asking for help. He even promised to give them some gifts if they could tell him the princesses' names. But they could not tell him because they did not know the princesses' names.

As the end of the seven days drew near, Tortoise became desperate. "What do I do now?" he asked himself. "Maybe I need to observe what the princesses do every day, their daily schedule. That may give me an idea," he thought.

For two days, Tortoise hung around the king's palace. Day and night, he hid in the woods that stood near the palace.

After two days of observation, Tortoise noticed the princesses got up together every night at the same time to use the toilet.

[Note that this was long ago, so the toilet was a pit latrine, a deep pit dug in the ground outside near to the house with a small hut built over it to protect it from the rain.]

Tortoise also noticed that there was light on the path from the princesses' bedroom to the toilet. But he thought the light was not bright enough.

That light had been there and that way since the time the

princesses were born. They never complained about it. They loved the way it was: not too bright and not too dark. For the princesses, the light was bright enough for them to see their way to the toilet and back to their room.

Tortoise found out the names of the Princesses

How did Tortoise do it? Next day, he went at night, before the hour the princesses usually used the toilet, and dug a shallow hole on the ground on the path leading from their room to the pit toilet in the backyard of the king's palace.

After doing that, he put himself into the hole, with his hump rising a bit from the ground. Thus, he stuck out one hand above the ground. For a good measure, he positioned his hand on the ground to make another bump. He also let his hump his back, stick out above the ground.

Soon, the princesses got up that night as usual to use the toilet. As they walked along the path, the first princess hit her foot against Tortoise's hand, tripped over it and fell down "whap" to the ground. As she fell, she shouted, calling out her name, "What is it that *Mma Mmama-a* is hitting her foot against?" [This princess may have been named after her mother's mother whose name was Mmama-a.]

The second sister was right behind the first one. She tried to help her, but she stubbed her toe on Tortoise's hump. She fell and landed on the ground next to the first sister.

The second princess cried, "What is it that hurts the toe of I, *who can only be married by someone who knows my name?*" She hurt her toe so badly that she got up limping.

As the first and second sisters were wailing in pain and looking around, trying to figure out what the bump was, the third sister, who was right behind the second one, shouted. She too knocked her foot against the same bump.

She fell over the bodies of the two sisters and landed flat on her back. She also screamed asking, "What is in the path of I, *He who tells my name will marry me?*"

The three princesses helped each other get up, walked to

the toilet, used it and went back to their room. As they walked back to their room, they made sure they did not go near to the bumpy spot that caused them to stumble, fall or limp.

"We have to tell our father, the king, in the morning about the unusual bump and the strange experience we had this night on the path to the toilet," the princesses decided. [The words in italics, the princesses called out were the names of the princesses.]

The princesses did not know the bumps on the path to the toilet were actually Tortoise's back and hand. But for Tortoise, he had cracked the mystery and got what he wanted: he found out the names of the king's daughters.

"Splendid," thought Tortoise, as he crawled home, feeling confident and well prepared to solve the king's puzzle and marry the three princesses.

Tortoise met with the king before day of contest

Tortoise was now very excited to get the king's daughters as his wives, and the gifts. So, he did not even wait until the day of the contest.

A day before the contest, Tortoise went to the king and said to him, "I know your daughters' names. I can tell you now if you want."

"You of all animals!" the king said in a loud voice. He was surprised. Why? "Hippo, Leopard, Elephant, Antelope, Cow and all other big animals came, but did not know my daughters' names."

Tortoise moved closer to the king and whispered one of the names into the king's ear, just to let the king know that he, Tortoise, knew the princesses' names.

"Do you know *all* the names or just one?" the king asked Tortoise.

"Oh! Long Live the King! I know them *all*," he told the king. And he bowed before the king as he told him that.

"If you are sure that you know *all* their names, you know

the custom and what to do," he reminded Tortoise.

"Yes, I already know it," Tortoise answered.

Tortoise pulled out a bottle of an expensive wine (or liquor) from his bag and gave it to the king. He asked the king for permission to discuss with him about marrying his daughters. That was what the custom required then, and up even till today in almost all Nigerian-Ibibio ethnic cultures.

"I like you as my son-in-law. I will let you marry my daughters, of course, only if you know their names," the king assured Tortoise.

Accordingly, the king accepted the wine, opened it and the two of them drank some, sipping it as they discussed the matter. "Do your part. I'll do mine," the king advised him.

Tortoise thanked the king and hurried back home to prepare for the D-day, the contest day coming up the next day.

Yes, Tortoise already knew marriage related customary practices. And fortunately, he found favor before the king during that visit to inform the king that he knew the princesses' names. He was lucky the king liked him and his family.

But if the king did not like him nor his family background for any reason, the king would not have opened the wine, and would have said to Tortoise, "Take your wine home. I have no daughter to give you to marry," (just as my father did to some of my suitors).

Tortoise publicly announced the princesses' names

The day of the contest came. It was also the wedding day for whoever would tell the names of the princesses. All the animals assembled at the king's palace.

The ceremony started. All the animals took turns as directed by the king in telling the names. Even those who failed in the past had another chance to try again. "Maybe, I will be lucky to get the names right this time," some of them thought. Still, they were not lucky, except Tortoise.

Tortoise was the last to go. With confidence, he stepped forward before the crowd as other animals did. He held up a cup of wine and called the name of the first princess, "*Mma Mmama-a,* come and take the drink."

She smiled. She stood up, walked toward him, and then got the drink and drank.

Everybody cheered at Tortoise. Some clapped hands. Some beat drums. Some sang. Some danced. Others jumped around, hailing him. Some fireworks sounded in honor of his cleverness.

Tortoise took another cup of wine, held it in his right hand and called the second princess by name, "*I, who can only be married by someone who knows my name* come and get this drink from my hand."

She got up, looked straight on Tortoise's face, walked toward him, took the drink and drank.

Drums and fireworks sounded again. There was a smile on everybody's face. It was not difficult to see 'happiness' on everybody's face. The princesses themselves smiled all over the place as if they had eaten some smiling medicine.

"What is the name of the third sister?" everybody asked in a loud voice.

Tortoise took another cup of wine and called out her name in a louder voice, "*I, who can only be married by someone who knows my name* come and get this drink."

She stood up, walked majestically, got the drink and drank it.

The people were shouting and praising Tortoise for being so clever. Singing, dancing, clapping of hands and fireworks did not stop.

Tortoise married the three princesses

Right after Tortoise had announced the princesses' names to everybody, the king did as he promised. He gave his three daughters to Tortoise to marry, and a lot of gifts to his daughters to take home with their husband.

There was merriment. The Wedding took place immediately. Everybody had fun. There was plenty of food for all and was more than enough. Some ate so much that they fell asleep on the dinner table and were snoring. Some ate until they could not get up to go home that day.

"What am I going to do with the surplus food?" the king asked. "Anyone who wants to take some left-over food home can do so," he gave permission.

Some animals did.

After Tortoise had announced the princesses' names, the king recognized Tortoise before all the animals as the cleverest and the most intelligent among all the animals in his kingdom.

Tortoise was happy, happy and happy for marrying the king's daughters, for all the gifts the king gave them, and the title.

The princesses were also happy to have a husband who was so intelligent.

The king was happy, as well, to have the smartest of all animals as his daughters' husband.

The people thanked Tortoise very much for revealing the names of the king's daughters to them. Before then, only the king and the queen knew their names. And not only that, the names of people in general were not in the public domain.

And from that day till today, names of people are no longer kept secret from other family members. Today, parents are freer than before to tell their children's names to other relatives and strangers who may ask with good intentions, and want to know, and of course, only if the parents feel safe doing so.

The great name-revealing ceremony changed the course of history of name-use practices in the world, according to Nigerian-Ibibio folklore. It was also one of the events that earned Tortoise respect, love and admirable reputation for being the most intelligent among animals and humans long ago, at a time when animals and humans were doing things together.

Who was not happy for Tortoise's overnight riches and fame?

All other animals were happy for Tortoise and rejoiced with him. But Leopard was not. He was jealous of Tortoise for all what he got from the king -- princesses as wives, great gifts, and the rare social recognition by the king as being the smartest, or the most intelligent, in the kingdom.

Leopard went home sad and very disappointed, and was determined to hurt Tortoise's family.

"I am going to eat up his wives," he said.

*　*　*

Moral Lesson:

Even when we seek a common good, how we obtain it must be as morally sound as the good itself.

What Tortoise did was a good thing. But how he set about it was morally questionable. However, that did not give Leopard permission or warrant him to be jealous to a point of hurting Tortoise's family.

Evidently, we shall see in subsequent volume where this story is continued, how one bad behavior led to another and to another.

Of course, Leopard and all those involved paid dearly for their destructive behaviors. So, every bad behavior has a consequence.

Emma Umana Clasberry has authored many books on African culture. Her works reflect some of the ideas birthed at a Chicago non-profit agency, African Peoples Institute she founded (1990s through 2000s), to promote cultural awareness and pride among youth and to aid them understand how knowledge of their ethnic culture or lack of it can impact their cultural identity, self-esteem and confidence, their education and career choices, and economic welfare and cultural pride of a people.

Emma has been a Subject of Biographical Record in *Who's Who of American Women*, 21st Edition, 1999/2000, for Significant Contribution to the Betterment of Contemporary Society.

She earned a B.A in Political Science and an M.A. in Urban Planning & Policy from University of Illinois at Chicago, and a Doctor of Education degree from California Coast University.

Other books by Emma: *Culture of Names in Africa...*; *African Culture Through Proverbs*; and more. Amazon; Xlibris.

ALIEN CAT

ROBERTA DAVIS

*T*ere she comes again. Hide! Hide, and food will magically appear. That's what Mom used to say. Where is Mom? It's bad enough she parties all night and comes home cranky. His siblings had vanished one by one. As for Mom, a couple full cycles of the sun went by since she went hunting. It felt like he had waited forever.

Lost in his pondering, the little black and white kitten peeked out from under the shed, testing the scents and sights. He saw the big two-legged alien walking away, making crunching sounds in the leaves that faded with distance. *Oh, it's the alien. Why is Mom scared of her? The alien smells of cats, but she doesn't have fur except for that long mane. Weird.*

A tasty aroma drifted to his sensitive nose. There was the food, but something was different. The flimsy white plates lay inside a strange contraption made of hard, straight, branches. It was like a tunnel you could see through.

Wow, for me? A jungle gym!

He'd play later. For now, there was food, and a game to find it. He munched up the scattered kibbles on the nearest paper plate, but the food ahead smelled much better. He glanced around, and saw nobody else. The food was all his! He edged farther in, giddy with luck, and his belly rumbling with hunger. Another little plate, with soft, yummy stuff, and another with a mother-load of great, smelly, wet food. *Yay!* He forgot about what his cranky mom taught him. This was all his food. Then he heard a click-thump. The jungle gym shifted a bit. *Huh?* He glanced around, and seeing no threat, resumed eating.

He was almost done when a familiar noise carried over

the forest of grass. The familiar, muffled thuds started crunching on leaves, growing louder as an ominous form lurked closer.

The big alien!

The kitten spun and bolted for the open hole, but the hard sticks had covered his exit. *What the? Lemme out!* "MEEOWWWW!"

So, this is why Mom warned him! It's a trap! She had dodged them for years, earning her the reputation as slickest cat in the hood. Sure enough, a shadow fell over his jungle gym and blocked out the sun. The whole contraption lifted, with him in it. "MEW? Oh, snap! HEEEELP!" He saw the ground moving beneath him until the world changed again, from the green forest to weird colors of a hard, smooth ground.

"MEOWW, HEELLLP! MEOWWW! Can't you understand cat? Lemme outta your stupid spaceship! I'm too little to eat!"

Miss Alien was talking to him, but her noises may as well be the famished growls of a wild dog.

Then the floor came up to meet his jungle gym and after an eternity of minutes, all went quiet. He didn't know whether to sulk or what. He tried digging, clawing, making up new awful names, but none of it worked. More scuffling started outside his portable den, and the end wall opened to a nice, cozy, hiding place. The kitten snuck into the dark chamber when another wall closed around him. *What! Are you serious? This one's even smaller!*

After a bit, Miss Alien opened his new den, and dared to try to groom him with a big, hairless paw. *The nerve! Steals me away and now touches me, O M G. Well, I'll only give name, rank, and serial number.* He laid down in full defense mode, jaw clenched shut. *Wait, what's that smell?* Something was hovering close to his head. *No way. I'm not falling for that again. I gotta get outta here! Fark, she's in my way.* Somehow, something crept past his lips, something wet. *Quit it! Yuck! What is that, fake milk? GROSS! I'm too old for your stupid milk. I can take care of myself. Grrr!*

A little dish of mushy meat stuff found its way into the dark little den, but he pointed his nose away from it. *Nope, ain't eatin' it this time. Maybe I can sneak away when it's dark.*

Despite his indignant refusals, Miss Alien was stubborn. The milk feeder kept taunting his taste buds, worse than a pesky sibling showing off a mouse.

Maybe it's a magic potion to brainwash me! Don't eat it! Lick, lick. *Ew, it's not Mom's.* His stomach was mean enough to battle his willpower. Maybe that warm, fake milk wasn't as good as Mom's, but it wasn't THAT awful, either. He sniffed the wet food. *Is that roadkill? Yum.* Still, pangs of reality gnawed at him. *Where are my brothers and sisters? Where is Mom? They left me! How could they?* Bitterly, he surmised they left him to this strange creature in a foreign world of shifting walls, magic tricks, and mysterious food.

After a bunch of arguments with the milk feeder, the kitten looked at the strange alien and something clicked. *Maybe she thinks she's a cat. That's the worst costume I've ever seen.* He nearly laughed. W*ell ... well...."You have milk and ground up critters? Wow."*

Tux slowly realized this wasn't so bad after all. Lick lick, nom nom nom. *This alien must be part cat. Maybe I can train her.*

Miss Alien and the vet were stunned when the four-month-old feral kitten decided to cuddle with her, after only two days inside. The kitten didn't care who said he was too old or too wild to tame. He made friends with the inside cats, and weeks later, he was playing fetch like a smart puppy.

After weeks went by, Tux saw his mama through the looking panes to the outside world. She looked like someone bit off the tip of her ear, but she was growing plumper and shinier. Cranky Serena looked good in her retirement. She and some of her kids from earlier families never came inside Tux's new world, but every so often, they would look in and wink at him.

Roberta "Bert" Davis has written fantasy and science fiction since childhood. She's a former Air Reserve Technician, and retired from the USAF Reserves as Master Sergeant after twenty-two years of service. A graduate of ERAU (Embry-Riddle Aeronautical University), her thesis was on Human Factors in Aircraft Maintenance. Roberta works as a lead technical writer by day, and writes sci-fi/fan by night.

Her first novel is in final edits with her editor (should be named the "100 Year Book" for taking so long.) She's published in the first two anthologies of SSWC (Sacramento Suburban Writer's Club"): *The Moving Finger Writes*, and *Thinking Through Our Fingers*, and NCPA's 1st Animal Anthology, *Birds of a Feather*.

Roberta is a lifelong animal enthusiast, learning from trainers and behaviorists much of her life. She volunteers some hours to Fieldhaven Feline Rescue and is a staunch supporter of animal and wildlife rescue.

Facebook: https://www.facebook.com/Dragonscriber.

ALONG CAME RYAN...THE LITTLE GOSLING KING

BARBARA KLIDE

A Coopers Hawk and a Gosling
April 20

We had heard her shrieks before, *kee-eeeee-arr, kee-eeeee-arr!* This time she was *not* announcing her presence. Tearing through the leafy canopies, the hawk's silence was menacing. One of fourteen raptor species in the Sacramento, California region, the Coopers Hawk's red eyes focused like lasers on a tiny, golden Canada Goose; a two-day old gosling with no feathers for flight. Even if it could fly, there would be no contest as the powerfully agile predator can reach a flight speed of 55 miles per hour.

Behind glass windows, several people watched in fear as the hawk emerged from the trees, racing for the open with her wings spread full and her legs out behind her. She dipped low for a split second, then startlingly swept away from the gosling, rocketing high and gliding over the building, out of sight.

On the lawn below, the baby's parents fiercely defended their offspring, honking with necks outstretched, and slapping their wings. On full guard, they tolerated no nonsense today. Everyone breathed a sigh of relief as the little goose family was now safe, but we knew the hawk would soon return to the enclosed courtyard, as her own nest of hungry chicks was located just outside it.

Only one gosling hatched after many eggs were laid. We called him Ryan like the actor, Ryan Gosling. It seemed momentarily funny, but it stuck. We endearingly named Ryan's Mom "Mother Goose", the imaginary author of children's nursery rhymes, often depicted as a goose. We named the male gander "Hawkeye"—like the lead actor in the TV series *Mash,* or the Marvel Comics superhero, or the protagonist in the book, *Last of the Mohicans*, take your pick.

Within 24 hours of hatching, goose parents lead their goslings to open water where they are able to dive and swim 30-40 feet underwater. Unable to fly out of the courtyard until he is two or three months old and fully fledged, little Ryan could not enjoy any lakes or rivers as he was plainly "landlocked." Still, life seemed sweet for the three of them with an automatic sprinkler system providing water and an abundance of grass for the geese, primarily vegetarians, to eat continuously.

My co-workers and I frequently stared out into the courtyard hoping to catch a glimpse of the wonderful little baby that was so full of life and impossibly cute. We fretted for the family's safety as the geese were "sitting ducks," so exposed and vulnerable, knowing that in one moment the possibility of death loomed large. Will the geese survive, let alone thrive?

The courtyard, the size of a soccer field, is encased on all four sides within a pair of connected buildings that house a 24' x 7' data center where I work, and a second business, also a tech firm. Canada Geese in flight, called a "skein" or geese in V formation, called a "wedge", fly over the building annually, north in spring and south in fall, signaling the changing seasons and for many, a sign of good luck.

From the sky, it may have seemed like a safe place, with its many shade trees around the perimeter, its vast lawn, and reliable source of water, for a mated pair of geese to nest but it was far from ideal.

Here is where our story actually begins…
Nesting
30 days earlier

For reasons known only to them, Mother Goose and Hawkeye decided to nest on the roof of a small structure, not unlike a bus stop with benches. Located along a wall inside the courtyard, it shelters workers from inclement weather and provides a place to enjoy the tranquil, fresh air setting. With no time to spare, nest building atop the structure began.

Only a few knew the geese had "landed", but word of it quickly spread. It was anybody's guess what material Mother Goose used to make the nest, but was likely the large fallen leaves, from the fruitless cherry tree branches above. The goose would then have created a soft nest lining with fuzzy feathers, or down, which she'd pull out from her chest. Whatever the construction, we all wondered about the anticipated set of eggs, a "clutch," that she would lay, and waited impatiently knowing that it takes some 30 days of incubation before they would hatch.

No one saw what happened next, but I suspected the hawk tried to steal the eggs, as I would often find broken eggs on the ground. The typical number of eggs geese lay is five or six, but she could have laid up to a dozen. Perhaps the predator dropped the snatched eggs after a bitter fight. I believed that if so, the geese would have battled to the last egg, and that's apparently just what they did.

Along Came Ryan
April 18

With great fanfare, along came Ryan! He was the only gosling to hatch. What a day that was! Goslings can walk within hours of hatching and the baby may have flown or fallen off the roof trying to follow his parents. With their fluff and small size, they can "flutter" down about two stories without injury; any higher and the goslings would have to be rescued.

Baby Ryan's appearance surprised and thrilled everyone. He was after all, a perfect little golden baby. We all started taking pictures left and right because he was, well, adorable and his photogenic parents were wildly majestic and graceful with their distinguished black heads and bill, long necks, and a striking white patch or "chinstrap."

From then on, Mom and Dad paraded the gosling around their private paradise, showing off little Ryan while rearing him in these secluded grounds.

Under normal circumstances, the goose and gander move the goslings to a "brood rearing area." Both parents take an active role in their care and protection. Often, several family groups rear brood flocks in the same vicinity called "crèches" where the parents teach the young geese, or "juveniles" to fly, taking off from both water and land. Constant practice with their wings outstretched, strengthens their young bodies, and helps them gain confidence.

How in the world Ryan would learn to fly in this unusual schoolyard was a mystery and became a growing concern.

Most days, Ryan delighted in the sunshine and the adoration of his mom and dad and sometimes stayed warm under Mom's wings in rainy or chilly weather. My co-workers and I admired the devoted parents and were completely captivated by the baby mascot, but when outside, we kept our distance to avoid Ryan inadvertently imprinting on us. Known to follow anything that moves, including dogs, ducks, and people, goslings are highly impressionable.

So mesmerized by the goose family, several staff frequently forgot to swipe their identification badges on the doors of the corridor paralleling the length of the courtyard. That meant a security alarm would go off—every time! Setting off the alarm, "set off" the security staff too, who rolled their eyes when called to reset the door alarm. The geese were such a novelty at the beginning that we suffered blaring alarms two or three times a day!

Then there was the other issue...maybe Ryan was a female! So, we figured, as an alternative, we could call the gosling Rihanna, like the singer—might as well have a celebrity female name to match the male actor's name. It should be pointed out that "Ryan" happens to be a classic Irish surname meaning "little king." That sealed the deal!

War
May 11

Early in the morning when I arrived at work, I saw a pair of geese on the entrance roof and my heart sank. That could only mean the baby was taken by the hawk and the parents had deserted the courtyard. After sharing the news, several of us made a beeline to the corridor. We looked out the windows while "badging" through the doors. Finally, as we flew through the last door, we all looked outside. To our immense delight, resting on a door mat safe and oblivious to our breathless fears, was the little family. Stunned, but happily so, I nearly cried for joy, but not all was calm.

No sooner were we filled with relief, when the geese jumped up in alarm. The parents charged toward the middle of the courtyard, the little one trailing them running as fast as his short little legs could take him. Now what? What could have disturbed the peace? So, we ran back yet again, following the action along the inside of the corridor. We tore through the locked doors, badging back in one-by-one, continually looking outside the windows for the answer. Very quickly, we found it.

Those two geese we saw on the roof, who we mistook for the parents, were invaders! They had flown off the roof and landed in the courtyard causing a major commotion for our little family. Geese are exceedingly territorial during the short nesting season and what we saw was a textbook display in action—war!

The adults began posturing, which is a precursor to battle. They were tearing towards each other and a vicious fight for dominance ensued amid hisses, snarls, growls, and deafening honks while they slapped each other with their strong wings.

Through the mêlée, the Gosling Ryan ran back and

forth, flapping his little wings a mile a minute copying his parents' moves. It occurred to us this might have been war lesson 101 for the baby. Either way, Mother Goose was also battling. She was on equal turf with her mate, Hawkeye. The fight went on for a good, long time until Mother Goose and Hawkeye successfully chased the invaders down to the south end of the courtyard. Just when we thought it was over, they clashed even more.

After persistent charging, the parents prevailed and at last, the invaders were chased into flight over the building in a dramatic, crushing retreat. Everything settled down rather quickly for the family. They shook off the intrusion with evident ease and began to snack on grass. Just another day in the life…meanwhile, I was inside worrying desperately for the family. Could they handle any more of these upsets? Could I? What was to come of them, and especially the baby?

Growing Strong
May 15

By May we saw the gosling transforming even faster. Over one weekend, when many of us were home, Ryan, the Little King, went from a soft downy baby to a teenager with the first appearance of tiny flight feathers right on schedule at approximately eight weeks! We thought about escorting him and his parents through the courtyard door to the other side, but there was no safe area or body of water on the grounds for them to finish raising the gosling. More importantly, he still couldn't fly.

…and Alone
May 22

We were just starting to feel less anxious about the little fellow as he was getting bigger, when one day, we realized with grave concern, the parents were gone! Where did they go, and why? We read that the parents occasionally go off to feed elsewhere, but will always return. To our utter happiness, by the end of the workday, they did. For a while, however, the parents would take off, one at a time, and sometimes the two would leave for many hours together. It became the norm, but we felt uneasy about this turn of events, especially since their time away stretched longer and longer.

As we continued to dig for more answers, we learned molting season was soon to start. The parents would lose all their flying feathers, which is an annual process, allowing geese to grow new feathers to replace those lost, frayed, or worn.

With his parents gone, little Ryan was often seen in repose alongside a shaded wall, contentedly eating, or strolling around. We worried that he was quite lonely, as geese are extremely social creatures, and prayed his parents would return soon to check on him.

By now, Ryan appeared to be completely abandoned, even though we read that geese parents will never do that. We thought they were waiting for him to fledge and be able to fly away with them, but the truth was, the parents started molting as expected, shedding feathers all around the courtyard. Instinctively, they knew when they had fully molted, they would not be able to fly (for 40 to 45 days), so they had to leave or stay and be stuck. What a dilemma!

I Can Fly
June 12

When Ryan was still little, an above-ground sprinkler was set up, separate from the system buried under ground to water the lawn. This new sprinkler became "their office water cooler" and the little family would head to it daily. It was endearing watching Ryan run to-and-fro in the water, flapping his wings. He would do so with such abandon that all our hearts leapt for joy.

Later, with his parents gone, our business neighbors delivered a kiddie pool to add to Ryan's pleasure, especially since the days were getting hotter. He swam and dunked under water, with his feet and tail feathers high in the air.

We made Ryan's world as amenable as we could – considering he couldn't be free in the wild. He was given a bucket of water for drinking, and after splashing around in his new pool he would hop out, shake off, and sun himself.

One person with a particularly soft heart for Ryan would seek him out, in the quiet of evening especially, when he seemed to go missing. She would look behind the trees and bushes and was always relieved when she'd find him. When he was simply chilling in his pool, she'd have a heart-to-heart conversation with him that went something like this, "Now listen little fella, this has gone on long enough. You need to learn to fly."

While he lacked guidance from Mother Goose, Ryan got help from Mother Nature. Amazingly, Ryan taught himself to fly! It was completely instinctive and mesmerizing. He would run from one end of the courtyard to the other gaining speed, and eventually would become airborne for a few seconds. Oh, what a big beautiful boy he was turning out to be! And yes, he could fly, but never away.

The Great Escape
July 13

On a Monday morning, a story began swirling. "He's gone! What do you mean, he's gone!?"

"Little Ryan has flown the coop! He went off with other geese." Could it be so?

I went across the courtyard to speak with some of the staff from the other company who, like us, were watching daily from their own windows. They too saw the Canada Geese activities unfold from the beginning, and I wanted to know if they had any new stories to tell. They mostly saw what we saw, but the hilarious thing about our parallel universes was we had both named the baby Ryan Gosling! We laughed together at that.

I did find that one lady with an office facing the courtyard had to chase the hawk away many more times than I realized. She could see the hawk's shadow while it was perching, and when she did, she tore into the courtyard to shoo the hawk away. Her concern was that in his growing independence, the gosling would waddle away from the parents. I'm almost glad I didn't know how often this happened, as I was worried enough for the baby.

Then I learned two of their staff had come in over the weekend to wash the swimming pool, which was on the south end of the courtyard. There, you can see through the glass breezeway beyond the courtyard to the outside of the building, where a small family of geese was lounging. Just a mom and six babies; no gander was evident. The babies were not really little. In fact, it was estimated they were only about one week younger than the Gosling Ryan.

On a snap decision, someone simply slid open the giant set of breezeway doors and tried to shoo Ryan through to meet up with this new family. We could have always let Ryan out the doors to freedom, but that was a frightening prospect, forbidden due to the proximity to the hawk's nest. Keeping him safe in his "nursery" seemed wise at the time. Either way, escorting Ryan through the breezeway at this wonderfully opportune moment was not going to be easy.

First, the mom and teens decided it was time to leave and they had to be herded back in a "wild goose chase." Then one of the staff managed to get Ryan through the first breezeway door, but Ryan was not convinced to continue. Each time he was walked forward on the carpeted floor, Ryan spun around and flew through the open door back into his courtyard nursery and the process had to begin all over again.

This went on half a dozen times until at long last he saw the returning goose family. Ryan excitedly charged forward to greet them, beyond the breezeway, while the second door was quietly pulled closed.

As it turned out, the teens were hotly complaining. Mom, on the other hand, instantly sized up the youngster and accepted him into her brood as if this was the most natural of things. And just like that, the Canada Geese took off waddling west into the sunset, but with a new member of their family in tow, and a human family left behind. My bereft heart only found relief when I came to realize this surrogate mom would lovingly teach little Ryan the rest of his lessons and he would never be alone again. It was the best possible ending.

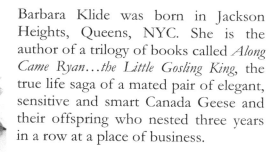

Barbara Klide was born in Jackson Heights, Queens, NYC. She is the author of a trilogy of books called *Along Came Ryan...the Little Gosling King*, the true life saga of a mated pair of elegant, sensitive and smart Canada Geese and their offspring who nested three years in a row at a place of business.

Barbara graduated from Golden Gate University, San Francisco, with a Masters of Business Administration degree and was awarded a Certificate in Graphic Design from the University of California, Extension, Davis. Her various careers in business include her current position of over 25 years as Director of Marketing for Quest Technology Management in Roseville, California.

She is a dedicated ballroom dancer at the Silver level through Arthur Murray International, Inc., Carmichael, California. Barbara and her longtime partner reside in Fair Oaks, California where they rescue, foster, and adopt out cats. Visit Barbara at: Barbaraklide.com.

NCPA * OUR PURPOSE * WHO WE ARE * WHAT WE DO

Northern California Publishers & Authors (NCPA) is an alliance of independent publishers, authors, and publishing professionals in Northern California.

Formed in 1991 as Sacramento Publishers Association, then expanded to Sacramento Publishers and Authors and eventually to NCPA, our purpose is to foster, encourage, and educate authors, small publishers, and those interested in becoming authors and publishers.

We support small indie presses, self-publishers and aspiring authors at our monthly meetings. by covering topics such as self- and traditional publishing, editing, book design, tax & legal issues, and marketing.

Service providers who cater to the publishing industry – illustrators, cover designers, editors, etc. – are also invited to join NCPA as associate members.

In addition to our annual NCPA Book Anthology, for *members only*, which started again in 2019, NCPA holds an annual Book Awards Competition for both *members, and non-members.* The NCPA Book Awards Competition celebrated our 25th year with 38 books published in 2018.

Check out our website www.norcalpa.org for information on our next Book Awards Competition, the next anthology and information on how to join NCPA.

NCPA also gives back to the community through proceeds from a Silent Auction during our Book Awards Banquets in the forms of: $1000 scholarship to a college-bound, local high school senior intending to pursue a publishing or writing-related degree; 916-Ink, which empowers youth through the published, written word; Mustard Seed School for underprivileged youth.

www.norcalpa.org

Made in the USA
Middletown, DE
09 November 2019

78131841R00109